Chakra

healing

Chakra

Using the body's subtle anatomy to balance and heal

healing

Sue Lilly and Simon Lilly

LORENZ BOOKS

This edition is published by Lorenz Books

Lorenz Books is an imprint of Anness Publishing Ltd
Hermes House, 88–89 Blackfriars Road, London SE1 8HA
tel. 020 7401 2077; fax 020 7633 9499
www.lorenzbooks.com
info@anness.com

© Anness Publishing Ltd 2002

This edition distributed in the UK by Aurum Press Ltd
25 Bedford Avenue, London WC1B 3AT
tel. 020 7637 3225; fax 020 7580 2469

This edition distributed in the USA and Canada by
National Book Network
4720 Boston Way, Lanham, MD 20706
tel. 301 459 3366; fax 301 459 1705; www.nbnbooks.com

This edition distributed in Australia by Pan MacMillan Australia,
Level 18, St Martins Tower, 31 Market St, Sydney, NSW 2000;
tel. 1300 135 113; fax 1300 135 103;
customer.service@macmillan.com.au

This edition distributed in New Zealand by David Bateman Ltd
30 Tarndale Grove, Off Bush Road, Albany, Auckland
tel. (09) 415 7664; fax (09) 415 8892

A CIP catalogue record for this book is available from the
British Library.

Publisher: Joanna Lorenz
Managing Editor: Helen Sudell
Senior Editor: Joanne Rippin
Designer: Nigel Partridge
Photographer: Michelle Garrett
Editorial Reader: Richard McGinlay
Production Controller: Claire Rae

10 9 8 7 6 5 4 3 2 1

This book is not intended to replace advice from a qualified medical
practitioner. Please seek a medical opinion if you have any concerns
about your health. Neither the authors nor the publishers can accept
any liability for failure to follow this advice.

Contents

introduction

Our lives are influenced by many different energies that we cannot see, and yet they can profoundly affect our state of mind and our health. We move within an invisible sea of electromagnetic energies, originating from the deepest regions of space and from the centre of our planet. Our personal space within and around our physical bodies is also inhabited by invisible but nonetheless powerful energies that, by their interactions, create and maintain our health. Perhaps the most important of these energies are located down the spinal column. Here, seven great vortices – called 'chakras', meaning 'wheels'– have been recognized by seers and healers for thousands of years as being essential to our wellbeing. Although most of us cannot see these chakras we can all learn to recognize how each one affects us at many different levels – physical, emotional, mental and spiritual.

Chakra healing seeks to understand the ideal creative energies that each chakra centre can bring to our lives and, by identifying where imbalances occur, help to restore our health. The most detailed examination of the chakra system is found in the teachings of ancient India. Oriental mysticism has attracted many people in the West who are interested in a different kind of spirituality from that offered by their own culture. Its ideas regarding healing are still viewed as unscientific by much of the Western medical establishment, but as more healers in the West come to understand the chakra system, this ancient knowledge is being successfully integrated into complementary therapies.

This book brings together a complex and involved philosophy, explaining it in such a way that everyone can benefit from the ancient healing legacy, and gentle power, of the chakras.

Overview of the Chakra System

'In the body there are many kinds of channels, which are very extensive. The sage must understand them in order to understand his own body… Running transversely, up and down, they exist in the body joined together like a wheel, dependent on the life-force and linked to the breath of the body.'

From the Shiva-Svarodaya Tantra, traditional Indian teaching on the subtle anatomy of the body.

What are chakras?

Over the last five thousand years, sages, philosophers and mystics have described the subtle energies in our environment and within our bodies in many different ways. Several systems have developed to explain them in the context of other philosophical backgrounds. However, it was generally agreed that wherever dynamic energies meet together in nature they form spinning circular patterns, or vortices. On a small scale this can be seen in tiny spiral eddies on the surfaces of streams and rivers; on a large scale in the movements of cloud systems that create cyclones and anticyclones.

The seers of ancient India perceived similar vortices within the energy of the human body. They described these in the Vedas, the primary source of all Hindu cosmology and philosophy, codified around 3000 BC. According to the Vedic seers, wherever two or more channels of subtle energy meet, there is a vortex, which they named 'chakra', meaning 'wheel'. Because these energy concentrations appeared to them to be funnel-shaped, multi-coloured and related to spiritual qualities, they became associated with the sacred lotus.

Where major energy flows coincide – on the midline of the body in the front of the spinal column – the seers of India saw seven main chakras that seemed to mirror both health and the spiritual state. These seven

△ **Wherever different streams of energy converge, a spiralling dynamic funnel, or vortex, is created, as in this cloud formation.**

chakras were like multi-dimensional gateways that would allow the individual to access different experiences and states of consciousness. The use of visualization, sound, chant, meditation and exercise to activate, cleanse and integrate these seven chakras became an important part of spiritual practice, especially in the Himalayan regions of India, Nepal and Tibet. Under guidance from an experienced teacher, each student was taught the appropriate methods to activate and integrate every part of the chakra system in a safe and balanced way.

Though everyone is likely to experience problems and energy stresses in different parts of the body and mind, our individual strengths and weaknesses are unique to us. In the same way, each chakra deals with particular areas of function, but the quality of the energy will vary from person to person. The skill of the teacher is to identify how to clear the energy pathways as the blocks reveal themselves.

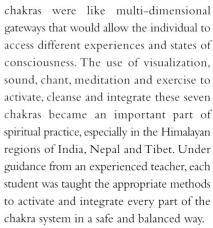

◁ **A depiction of the body's chakras and energy channels from an 18th-century Hindu manuscript.**

△ The spirals of nature mirror the vortices in the human body, which are formed when two or more channels of energy meet.

▽ The Vedic seers could perceive the structure of the cosmos and had startling knowledge of its true nature. In the same way, they were able to understand how cosmic energies manifested themselves within the human body.

chakras today

Many of the original Vedic texts discuss the development of psychic skill and supernatural power that arises from spiritual exercises. This connection with the spirit world attracted the attention of 19th-century Western thinkers, many of whom had become interested in oriental mysticism. As movements such as Spiritualism and

Theosophy developed, the Vedas were translated into Western languages. These translations emphasized the development of the higher chakras, and the desire to go beyond, or escape from, the bonds of the physical world. This bias echoed the trends of theosophical thinking, and usefully avoided what were viewed as embarrassing sexual techniques involving the three lower chakras. This false division into lower (or mundane) and higher (or spiritual) chakras misses the point that is continually reiterated in the original texts: that all chakras are of equal practical value.

Today our way of understanding the chakras is different again. Since the 1970s the seven chakras have been seen as fitting in with the other sets of sacred sevens, and have become particularly associated with the seven rainbow colours, with each chakra having its own colour. Although this is a modern departure it works very well, combining as it does an easy-to-remember colour code with the qualities and functions of each chakra. It is important to remember, however, that whichever system is used, classical or modern, it is really no more than a partial description of a complex set of energy interactions that make up the human mind, body and spirit.

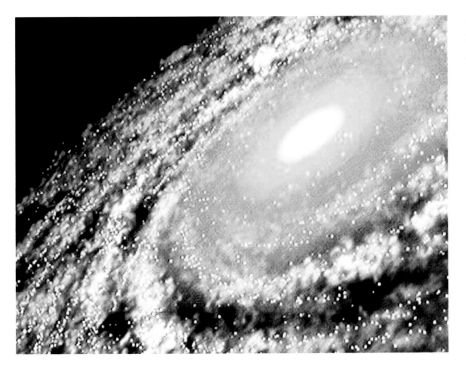

Chakra imagery

Whatever their correlation to physical structures within the body, chakras are entirely non-physical. The mind, rather than the sense organs, is the traditional tool for accessing, exploring and balancing the energy of each chakra. The main features of each chakra are described here as in the original Vedic texts, as they would be visualized by a meditator. Each chakra is symbolized by layers of imagery, including a particular animal, and a god and a goddess whose form and attributes encapsulate the inherent qualities that arise when the chakra is functioning in a balanced way.

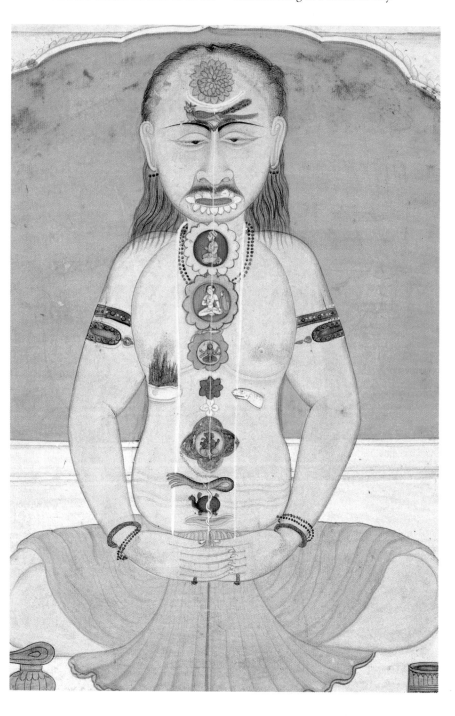

muladhara

This is the base chakra and its name means 'foundation'. It has four vermillion petals around a yellow square. The yellow square represents the element of Earth and the petals represent the four directions: north, south, east and west. The animal form representing the base chakra is a seven-trunked elephant, associated with solidity and assuredness. The elephant's trunks represent the sacred sevens, the chakras, planets, colours, notes and behavioural aspects which each of us must work with in the world. On the elephant's back rests the bija, or seed, mantra – the sound that stimulates the energy of this chakra – Lam. The god and goddess images show attributes of fearlessness and stillness.

svadistana

The sacral chakra, whose name means 'sweetness', has six red petals. It represents the Water element. The sacral chakra's animal is a crocodile, which represents its sensuous, watery and deceptively strong energy. On the crocodile rests the bija mantra Vam. The images of the god and goddess display peaceful emotions.

manipura

The solar plexus chakra's name means 'city of gems'. Ten luminous blue petals surround a downward-pointing red triangle, symbol of the Fire element. The animal is a ram: headstrong and direct, his fiery nature controls the group of which he is the leader. The deities represent control over anger and control of energy. The bija mantra is Ram.

anahata

The name of the fourth, or heart, chakra means 'unstruck'. Twelve deep red lotus petals surround a hexagram or six-pointed star of grey-green, representing the element

◁ **An Indian depiction of the chakras, each with their god or goddess within.**

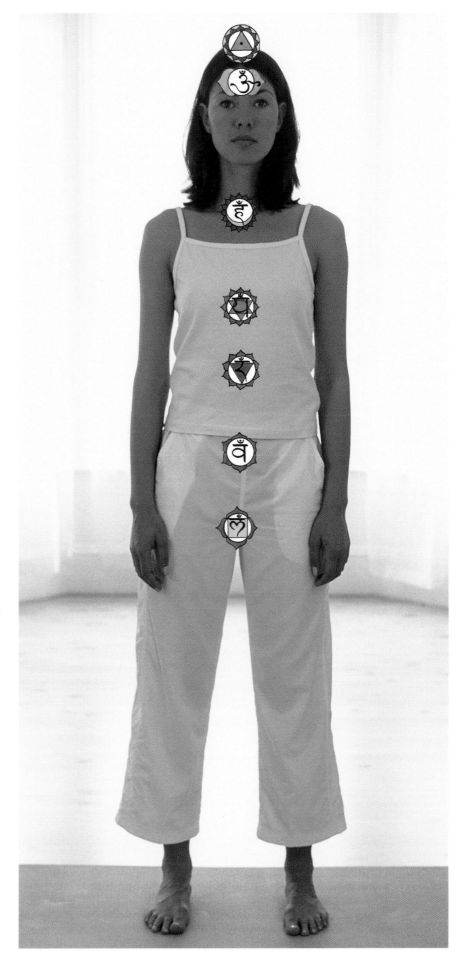

of Air. The animal is a black antelope, leaping with joy. It shows the sensitive, aware and curious nature of the heart chakra. On the back of the antelope rests the bija mantra Yam. The sound here controls breath and life-energy. The deities represent the arts and harmony in both inner and outer worlds.

vishuddha

This is the throat chakra, and its name means 'pure'. It has a circle of 16 lavender or smoky purple petals enclosing a silver crescent and the white circle of the full moon. This represents the ether or space, where all the elements dissolve into their refined essence, akasha, the pure cosmic sound. The animal is an elephant, the colour of clouds. His single trunk represents sound and he carries the memory of all past knowledge. He carries the bija mantra Ham, which empowers his voice. The deities represent the union of the elements, dreams of inspiration and higher knowledge.

ajña

The brow chakra's name means 'command'. It has two petals of luminescent pearly blue. Within a white column (the 'colour of light') is a representation of unified consciousness – a combined male and female deity. There is no animal here for the bija mantra, Aum, to rest on, so it rests on the finest quality of sound itself, known as nada. The goddess of this chakra embodies unconditional truth.

sahasrara

The 'thousand-petalled' crown chakra is at the top of the head. It is sometimes described as formless, sometimes as a moonlike sphere above which is an umbrella of a thousand petals with all the colours of the rainbow. The bija mantra is the 'nng' sound, known as Visarga. This is the breath-like sound that ends all previous bija mantras. It rests upon the bindu, the first moment of creation in the relative universe.

Physical correspondences

Because they cannot be seen by normal means, the chakras and the nadis – their related system of subtle channels – are represented by diagrams and other symbolic maps of the body. This is necessary to clarify the relationship between the subtle centres and the physical organs and structures with which we are familiar. However, mapping the chakras in this way can lead to a very static, inflexible and two-dimensional view of what is an elegant, dynamic and ever-changing interaction of energies.

Being non-physical, influencing matter but not consisting of matter, chakras are not bound by the laws of matter. In classical texts the chakras and nadis are considered to be expressions of consciousness. Time and

▽ A diagrammatic view of the chakras helps to identify their physical correspondences, though it does not reflect their interactive nature.

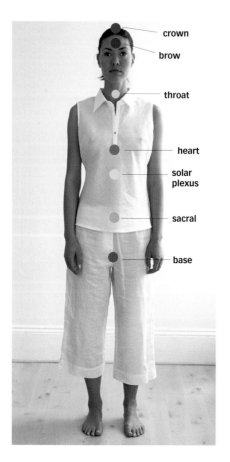

- crown
- brow
- throat
- heart
- solar plexus
- sacral
- base

△ Chakras provide the underlying orderliness of our being. Those with clairvoyant sight see them at every level, from physical to most subtle.

space, three-dimensional existence and scale have little relevance, except as a way to understand the chakras in familiar terms.

Around each chakra, echoing its function, are one of the main endocrine glands, a concentration of nerves known as a plexus, and concentrations of blood vessels and lymph nodes. There is some difference of opinion as to which physical system is related to which chakra, but most healers follow the correspondences described below.

the base chakra
Located at the base of the spine, the base chakra is sometimes represented as a vortex with a downward opening. In some systems it is related to the testicles or ovaries, in others to the adrenal glands. Although physically a long way from the base, the adrenal glands reflect the survival instinct of this chakra. The concentration of nerves in this area is called the coccygeal plexus.

the sacral chakra
The second chakra, sometimes called the sex chakra, is located in the lower abdomen, between the navel and the pubic bone. It is related to the sacral vertebrae in the spine, the sacral plexus of nerves and the sex glands – the ovaries and testicles. This chakra is associated with emotions and sensuality.

the solar plexus chakra
The third chakra is located on the front of the body between the bottom of the ribcage (diaphragm) and the navel. It is concerned with personal energy and power and is associated with the adrenal glands and the pancreas. The solar plexus chakra is named after the complex of nerves found here and is connected to the lumbar vertebrae.

THE LIMBIC SYSTEM

Deep in the centre of the brain lies a complex series of organs known as the limbic system. Within it, the pineal and pituitary glands control all the hormone systems of the body – in the same way that the crown chakra regulates the chakra system. Modern Vedic seers have linked each part of the limbic system with the functions and energies of the planetary influences in our lives: microcosm and macrocosm can exist at the level of neuroscience, as can the concept of the non-physical chakras.

▽ **The pineal (left) and pituitary, or master, gland (right) are very small organs that control the body's hormone-releasing systems.**

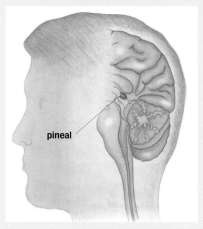
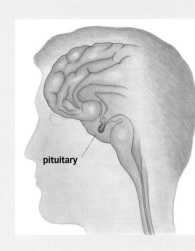

the heart chakra

The fourth chakra is the heart, located in the centre of the chest, associated with the thoracic vertebrae of the spine. The related gland is the thymus, a small gland above the heart vital for growth and the maintenance of the immune system. Two nerve centres are found here – the pulmonary plexus and the cardiac plexus. This chakra deals with love and relationships.

the throat chakra

The fifth, or throat, chakra is located near the cervical vertebrae and the base of the throat. It manifests communications and creativity. The thyroid and parathyroid glands (which control the body's metabolic rate and mineral levels) and the pharyngeal plexus are found here.

the brow chakra

The sixth chakra is the brow, located in the centre of the forehead. This is linked to the pineal gland that maintains cycles of activity and rest, and to the carotid plexus of nerves. The brow chakra directs intuition, insight and imagination.

the crown chakra

The seventh chakra, the crown, is located just above the top of the head and influences all the higher brain functions. It is connected to the pituitary, the gland that controls the whole endocrine (hormone) system. The entire cerebral cortex is influenced by this centre. The crown is associated with knowledge and understanding.

subtle forces

The modern study of embryology has yet to uncover the mechanisms by which original cells, which are identical and undifferentiated, migrate to certain places in the embryo and begin to form specialized organs. In complementary medicine and the holistic philosophies of non-Western cultures, it is the unseen, subtle forces, or spiritual powers, that control the existence of physical matter.

Like seed crystals dropped into a saturated solution, concentrations of dynamic orderliness, or points of consciousness, act as a template for the accretion of physical matter and the development of the systems of the human body. The chakras can be understood as working in the same way as planetary bodies in a solar system. Each, by its placement and qualities, attracts free floating matter and maintains it in its orbit.

Seen as concentrations of consciousness or crystallized mind, the physical systems of the body cannot be separated from the subtler structures. The body, mind and emotions are all extensions of chakra function. Changes at one level will bring automatic changes at every other level. Dysfunction at the physical level is echoed in the function of the chakras, and stress in the chakras can be felt as discomfort at the level of mind, body or emotion.

▷ **The endocrine glands maintain hormone balance in the body. Energy levels, emotional states and reactions to external and internal conditions are under their direct control. They can be seen as representatives of the chakras at a physical level.**

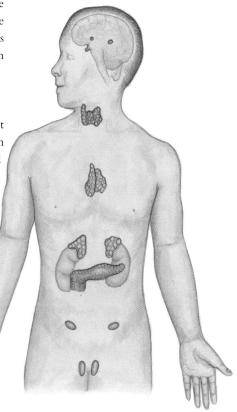

Cycles of nature

In the original Indian texts the chakras are related to a series of milestones in life. Each chakra and its function represent a stage of development and growth. Each stage can be seen as a time in which certain skills are developed. The precise shift from one stage of development to another will vary from individual to individual. The stages may overlap, but in some cases, where stress or trauma disrupts the chakra energy, this may create an underlying problem for subsequent growth. If one function remains underdeveloped, all the others dependent on it will have a built-in dysfunction.

conception and birth

The base chakra relates to the creation of the physical body, so it represents a stage of growth that begins at conception and continues until around the age of one year. The immediate, powerful energy of the base chakra is evident in the speed of growth and the primary need to survive. An infant during this time is dependent on others for its food, warmth and shelter. This period helps to anchor the individual into the physical world.

the developing baby

The sacral chakra begins to activate consciously at about six months and its effects last to around the age of two years. The feedback in this time comes from pleasure and gratification. The distinction between the child and the mother begins to become more apparent. Being given space to explore existence without negative reinforcement or verbal reprimand helps to build confidence in being a separate individual.

▽ All chakras are present in the growing child but during natural development energy focuses at certain centres.

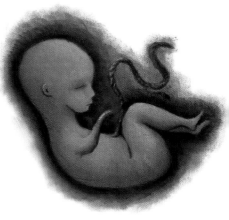

◁ From the moment of conception, consciousness coalesces around the energy of the chakras. The primary needs of survival and nutrition are the first focuses of each new life.

the small child

The onset of the activity of the solar plexus chakra is commonly referred to as the 'terrible twos'. It starts at around 18 months and lasts until the child is about four years old. This is when language develops, together with an understanding of the passing of time. Maintaining the balance between freedom and discipline is crucial at this age. Lack of restraining discipline creates an overpowering, egotistic child, whereas too much control will stop any sense of autonomy developing.

the child

The heart chakra covers the period from four to seven years and is characterized by relationships outside the immediate family. Relating helps to build self-esteem and self-acceptance. If love and relationships are always seen as being conditional – that is,

▽ Shared, cooperative creativity flourishes when the sacral and throat chakras have developed in a balanced way. Problems can arise if other chakras do not work in harmony.

having an emotional price-tag attached – the underlying feelings of guilt and grief caused by not receiving enough love can create great difficulties through life.

the pre-pubescent

The development of the throat chakra between the ages of seven and 12 marks the beginning of the stage of self-expression. If the lower chakra energies have been integrated to a reasonable extent, confidence can be gained from a firm emotional base. Through the throat chakra, this is given back to the community and family, sometimes in plays and perfomances.

the adolescent

The brow chakra covers the adolescent years, when the young person should be encouraged to reflect on the patterns in their own and others' lives. This is the first of several key stages when it is possible to re-invent and readjust the role that an individual sees themselves playing in the world.

the adult

The crown chakra becomes active between 20 and 27 years, as the individual fully reacts and interacts with the world. Sometimes this stage stays dormant, because it relates to questions like 'Why am I here?' and statements like 'There must be more to life than this.' These issues may never be looked at. On the other hand, the action of exploring them may be the beginning of a radical change of life and work. Having gone through a whole cycle, the

◁ Play exercises all the chakras, no matter what the age: it fosters a sense of security, energy, a desire to explore, confidence, ability to relate to the world, self-expression and imagination.

process begins again with the base chakra. Just as, in musical scales, each octave returns to the start note, the chakra cycle can repeat many times in a single life. The fact that this cycle renews itself periodically gives us opportunities to heal and repair ourselves. This enables us gradually to strengthen the energy within our chakra system and express more of our potential.

▷ As adults, we pass through successive cycles of the chakra system, continuing our own spiritual growth while also perhaps fostering the development of children.

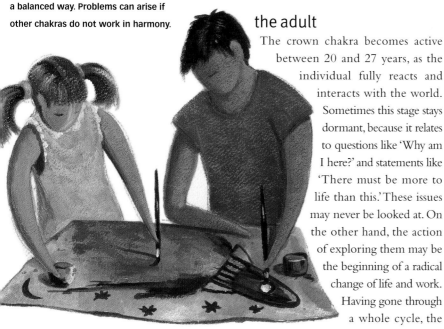
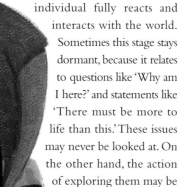

Nadis, kundalini and minor chakras

The seven main chakras are only part of a much larger complex of subtle energies that make up the individual human being. For example, there are many other chakras throughout the body, all of which are expressions of different kinds of consciousness and energy. The physical disciplines, such as hatha yoga – the use of specific postures to encourage spiritual development and health – and mudra – the holding of specific hand positions – have developed to make use of the energy of these smaller chakras and the channels that link them together.

Surrounding each chakra are the main channels of energy, called nadis, that flow from the centre and interact with the rest of the body. Nadis are related to some aspects of the autonomic nervous system, and also to the meridian channels identified in traditional Chinese medicine, but they are of a much finer subtle substance.

There are said to be, in total, 72,000 nadis. Fourteen are named and described in detail, and of these three are of prime importance: the ida, the pingala and the sushumna. These three main channels run parallel to the body's physical axis of the spinal column.

The sushumna is the central channel, and the most important. This is the channel that yogis seek to cleanse and into which they direct energy to achieve realization. As the Tibetan teacher Lama Sangwa said: 'By causing the winds (pranas) and subtle drops (elements) to enter into the central channel, bliss arises and the body itself becomes the source of enlightened awareness.'

Ida, the left channel, carries a lunar energy that is nourishing and purifying.

▽ This traditional image, called Sri Chakra, is a schematic representation of the main energy components of the human body.

▷ The Sushumna is the central channel from which the chakras emerge. Weaving from side to side are the Ida and Pingala, the sun and moon channels.

▷ The caduceus represents the Staff of Hermes, the Greek Messenger of the Gods. It was adopted as the symbol for healing and bears a striking resemblance to the three main nadis of the human body.

△ **The lotus petals round each chakra represent the nadis that distribute that chakra's energy through the body. Each chakra and nadi are expressions of the individual's core life-energy held within the three central channels.**

NADI SODHANA

Purification of physical and subtle energies in the body helps to clear the nadis, strengthens the chakras and begins to free up the primal energy of kundalini. A safe, well-balanced exercise for this is a breathing exercise (or pranayama) known as nadi sodhana. This exercise helps to balance the energy in the left and right channels (ida and pingala) and is calming and relaxing.

1 Sit comfortably with a straight spine. (If sitting in a chair, plant your feet flat on the floor.) Tuck your chin in so that the back of your neck is straight. Sit for a moment with your hands on your knees and calm your body and mind.

2 With the right ring finger, close off your left nostril by gentle pressure to the fleshy part and inhale slowly and deeply through the right nostril.

3 Now use your right thumb to close the right nostril, releasing the left nostril, breathing out through the left nostril, slowly and deeply.

4 Keep the right thumb in place and now breathe in through the left nostril. At the end of the breath, close the left nostril with the right ring finger again.

5 Now breathe out slowly through the right nostril.

6 Repeat the whole sequence of breaths ten times.

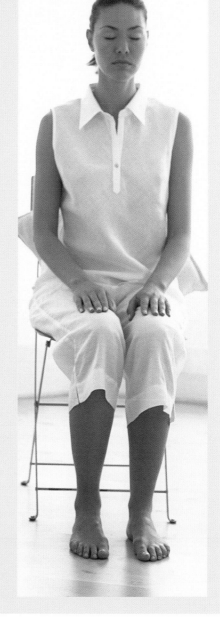

Pingala, the channel on the right side of the sushumna, is said to carry solar energy. The three channels are sometimes represented as running parallel to each other, while in other depictions the solar and lunar channels are seen weaving between the chakras until all three meet at the brow chakra.

The fundamental life energy of the individual is thought to reside in a quiet state within the base chakra. This force is called kundalini, which means 'coiled up'. As the chakras and their nadis are cleansed of stress and other energy blockages, more of the kundalini energy is able to move freely through the body. As this energy is pure consciousness, its awakened state can create various degrees of realization or enlightenment in the individual.

Many of the main chakras located on the central channel have smaller associated energy centres. For example, the muladhara at the base of the spine has related centres at the groin points, the knees and the soles of the feet. All these minor chakras help to ground and balance the physical energies. The heart chakra, anahata, has a smaller chakra inside it, which is represented as having eight petals. This is the spiritual heart, the anandakanda, whose eight channels represent the emotions.

Chakras in other therapies

Although the chakras are non-physical, they influence physical functioning. Their subtle channels, the nadis, interface with many systems, both energetic and material.

The original theory of the chakras was holistic. It set out a coherent system of psycho-spiritual development that automatically included the health and wellbeing of the physical body. Blocks and stresses caused by ignorance and inappropriate belief systems were believed to produce physical illness and spiritual suffering. Nowadays, complementary and alternative therapies are again seeking to work with a unified holistic vision of the human being. For this reason, integrated and self-contained systems like the chakras are again becoming useful models for healing.

yoga

Followers of the original Indian spiritual traditions worked with the chakra energies through physical exercise. Hatha yoga

▽ Hatha yoga is effective because it directly influences the chakra system. Holding a posture ensures that the nadis, the chakras and the muscles all work to bring specific functions of the system into balance.

positions (asanas) are designed to tone the physical body and stimulate the chakras and their nadis. They will do this automatically, though it is useful to follow a sequence of asanas that works through each of the chakras in turn.

sound

Used to restore balance to the body, sound therapy is often focused on the chakras. Each area of the physical system is made up of different densities of tissue and hollow cavities. Sound, either produced externally by a therapist or internally by the patient, resonates with different areas of the body according to the tone that is being made. Blocks in the emotions, the physical body and within the chakras can be loosened and released very effectively by sound. Resonant instruments such as didgeridoos, tuning forks, bells, gongs and singing bowls can all be placed close to chakra points.

Toning, which uses the resonant voice to make particular sounds, is also commonly used to release blocks. For example a resonant 'mmm' sound vibrates the bones of the head and the brow chakra, while an open 'aaah' sound relaxes the diaphragm and energizes the solar plexus.

△ Sound vibrates the physical structures of the body, and its subtle qualities also help to balance or clear the chakras and nadis.

▽ Colour therapy harnesses light, the subtlest of all physical energies. Specific colours can be used to help energize and heal particular chakras.

colour therapy

The original yogic exercises placed great emphasis on visualization. This often involved building up exact and powerfully coloured shapes and patterns, each of which created specific changes within the brain function and caused energy channels to activate around particular chakras.

Today colour therapy offers healers a valuable way of working directly with chakras. There are many ways of introducing colour into the human energy system. Shining coloured light directly on the chakra, over the whole body or through the eyes all create physical, emotional and mental changes. Visualization and imagination techniques involving colour are also often used. The body affects the mind and the mind affects the body, and as the ancient yogis and seers of all cultures discovered, energy flows where the attention of the mind is directed. This energy is the same as prana, or life-energy, so naturally it can be effective in bringing health to an area needing attention.

▽ **Crystal therapy uses the combination of colour and resonance – the energy unique to each type of stone – to rebalance the chakra centres.**

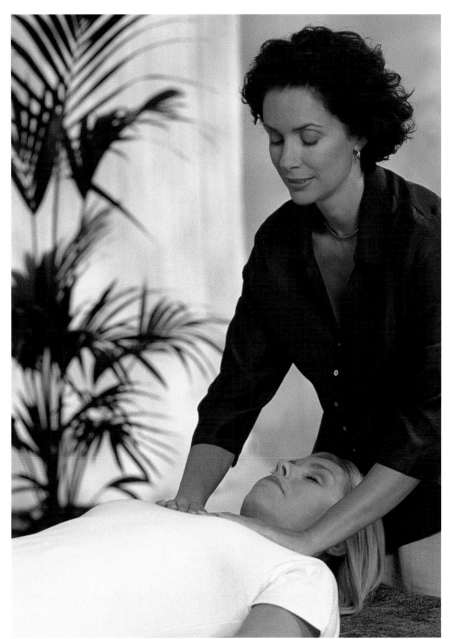

△ **Even therapies that do not specifically focus on the main chakra points have a profound influence on them. Any release of stress takes the burden off the chakra system as a whole.**

crystal healing

In crystal healing the seven main chakras are often the primary areas of stone placement. The organized structure of natural minerals has been found to have a beneficial and quick-acting effect on balancing the chakras. After an initial assessment, during which the quality of energy in each chakra is determined, stones are placed on and around each centre. The stones very often follow the Western colour correspondences, so that red stones will naturally enhance the qualities of the base chakra, orange stones those of the sacral chakra, and so on. From this starting point the therapist can modify the approach to release stress and correct under- and overactive chakra states.

healing by touch

Spiritual or hands-on healers may focus their healing attention at chakra points where they sense energy flowing with a significantly greater or lesser intensity than elsewhere. Because chakras are energy gateways that allow a flow of energy both inwards and outwards, they are natural focuses for a great many developing types of holistic therapy.

Discover your own chakra energy

Chakra energies are forever changing, interacting, balancing and rebalancing. From hour to hour and minute to minute as our activities alter, we move from concentration, to remembering, to physical coordination skills, to relaxing. As we do so, different chakras become more or less dominant. As individuals we each have a predisposition to certain chakras being more dominant than others. If we enjoy physical activity and have a practical, hands-on job, this will focus our energies at the first and second chakras. On the other hand, with an occupation that focuses on organizational skills and ideas, the solar plexus and brow chakras will inevitably become more significant.

Our life circumstances also alter the flow and interactions the chakras have with each other and with the environment. For example, if we are naturally comfortable working in socially complex interpersonal relationships – a heart chakra state – and then have to spend time where there is little chance to interact with others, or where our relationship skills are not valued, then this inevitably requires us to 'change gear' and focus our chakra energies in different ways. If we can identify the chakras that need

▽ **Give yourself time to think about the questions before you choose your answer.**

balancing, we can help ourselves a great deal in our journey towards our full potential and wellbeing.

Chakra dominance is not in itself a problem. However, where a major imbalance occurs, one or more chakras begin to take over the roles more properly belonging to others. This overburdens the dominant chakras and atrophies the others. We can survive for a long time in this false equilibrium, but it is like having a toolkit where only the hammer is used whatever the job. Often it is an accumulation of stresses and trauma in a chakra that reduces its effectiveness. If this is not remedied the system will naturally compensate by diverting energy to areas that are still working. This is the state of false equilibrium that most people cope with in their lives.

the questionnaire

In the following questionnaire there are seven options open to you for each question posed. Jot down the number of each reply on a sheet of paper. Pick more than one choice if it seems appropriate.

Now see how many times you recorded each number. Each refers to a chakra: 1 the base chakra, 2 the sacral chakra, 3 the solar plexas chakra, 4 the heart chakra, 5 the throat chakra, 6 the brow chakra and 7 the crown chakra. If you look at your score, you will be able to see which chakras are dominant for you.

For example, if you have two answers of number 1, two of 2, six of 3, two of 4, three of 5, one of 6 and three of 7, you will see that the third chakra, the solar plexus, is dominant. This is where most of your energy is focused. Although dominant, the solar plexus chakra needs the most attention and healing. Chakras 1, 2 and 6 (base, sacral and brow) have little focus of attention, so they too, may need healing and energizing.

▷ **If some of your chakras are overburdened your system will not be functioning properly.**

THE QUESTIONNAIRE

1 Which area(s) of your body concern you the most?
❶ feet and legs
❷ between waist and hips
❸ waist
❹ chest
❺ neck and shoulders
❻ face
❼ head

2 Which area(s) of your body do you dislike?
❶ feet and legs
❷ between waist and hips
❸ waist
❹ chest
❺ neck and shoulders
❻ face
❼ head

3 Which area(s) of your body are you proud of?
❶ feet and legs
❷ between waist and hips
❸ waist
❹ chest
❺ neck and shoulders
❻ face
❼ head

4 Which area(s) of your body are affected by major health issues?
❶ feet and legs
❷ between waist and hips
❸ waist
❹ chest
❺ neck and shoulders
❻ face
❼ head

5 Which area(s) of the body are affected most by minor health issues?
❶ feet and legs
❷ between waist and hips
❸ waist
❹ chest
❺ neck and shoulders
❻ face
❼ head

6 Which colour(s) do you like the most?
❶ red
❷ orange
❸ yellow
❹ green
❺ blue
❻ dark blue
❼ violet

7 Which colour(s) do you like the least?
❶ red
❷ orange
❸ yellow
❹ green
❺ blue
❻ dark blue
❼ violet

8 Which are your favourite foods?
❶ meat/fish/pulses
❷ rice/orange fruits
❸ wheat/yellow fruits
❹ green fruit and vegetables

9 Which sort of exercises or interests attract you?
❶ fast action
❷ dancing/painting
❸ crosswords/puzzles
❹ anything outside
❺ drama/singing
❻ mystery/crime novels
❼ doing nothing

10 What sort of people do you look up to or admire?
❶ sportspeople
❷ artists/musicians
❸ intellectuals
❹ conservationists
❺ speakers/politicians
❻ inventors
❼ mystics/religious figures

11 What sort of person do you think of yourself as?
❶ get on with things
❷ creative
❸ thinker/worrier
❹ emotional
❺ chatterbox
❻ quiet
❼ daydreamer

12 What emotions do you consider are uppermost in you life?
❶ passionate
❷ easy-going
❸ contented
❹ caring, sharing
❺ loyal
❻ helpfully distant
❼ sympathetic

13 What emotions do you have that you would like to change?
❶ temper
❷ possessiveness
❸ confusion
❹ insecurity
❺ needing things to be 'black or white'
❻ feeling separate from others
❼ not saying 'no'

14 If you get angry, what is your most common reaction?
❶ rage/tantrums
❷ sullen resentment
❸ get frightened
❹ blame yourself
❺ keep quiet
❻ withdraw
❼ imagine nothing happened

15 What are you most afraid of?
❶ dying
❷ lack of sensation
❸ things you don't understand
❹ being alone
❺ having no-one to talk to
❻ losing your way
❼ difficult situations

16 Which of these describes the way you prefer to learn?
❶ fast
❷ slowly
❸ quickly but forget
❹ through feelings
❺ by rote
❻ instinctively
❼ can't be bothered

17 What best describes your reaction to situations?
❶ enthusiastic
❷ go with the flow
❸ think things through
❹ see how things feel
❺ ask a lot of questions
❻ see the patterns then act
❼ drift along

18 If you are criticized or reprimanded, what is your usual response?
❶ anger
❷ resentment
❸ fear
❹ self-blame
❺ verbal riposte
❻ think about it
❼ denial

19 How would you describe your favourite books, films, video games?
❶ combat action
❷ art
❸ skill, intellectual
❹ romances
❺ courtroom dramas
❻ detective stories
❼ spiritual or self development

20 Which category best describes your friends?
❶ competitive
❷ creative
❸ intellectual
❹ loving
❺ idealistic
❻ rebellious
❼ spiritual

The Chakras of Manifestation

Once you have completed the questionnaire on the previous page you can use the following chapters to find appropriate ways to heal and balance the chakras that need attention. This chapter covers the first two chakras, the base and the sacral. They ensure the stability of the individual at every level of body, mind and spirit.

Base chakra – foundation of energy

Matter requires stability and structure in order to exist. Energy must be organized and maintained in the face of all sorts of opposing forces in the universe. The force of gravity is the energy of compression and its focus is the basis of the first chakra, located at the bottom of the spine. This is the rock upon which the whole of the chakra system, the subtle energies and the physical body rely, and without which disorder soon arises.

The Sanskrit name for the base chakra is muladhara, which means 'root'. The foundation of our life is the physical body

▽ **The muladhara chakra ensures our physical existence, nourishing and energizing the whole chakra system.**

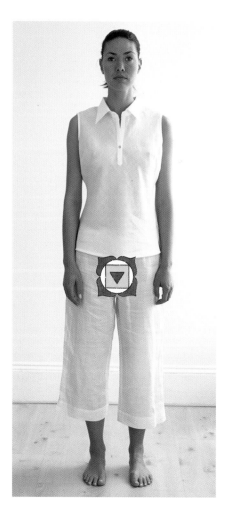

△ **Placing too much value on thought processes, of knowing rather than feeling, can create an imbalance that isolates us from the planet.**

and its ability to use energy to sustain itself. Survival is the key activity of the base chakra, which deals with life at the level of practicality. The base chakra is the closest energy centre to the Earth and it links us to the planet itself.

head in the clouds

The base chakra is what links 'us' – the consciousness sitting up there in the head commenting on everything that's going on – with our bodies. Many ancient cultures saw the mind or soul as located in the heart. The West puts emphasis on the head, the seat of the rational thinking mind, and often views the body as an awkward nuisance. With such a dissociation, the natural connections with physical reality and the sense of being a part of creation can be lacking. This induces a false sense of detachment, disinterest or even disdain, where nothing is truly valued and nothing is appreciated. Life can quickly become dull and meaningless.

△ **Our sense of self, and desire to live, are the hidden roots of our existence; this is the ground of our being that sustains us constantly.**

reactions

The base chakra relates to physical solidity and support, especially to the skeletal structure of the body and its flexibility. It is no use having a strong physical base if there is no flexibility. In order to survive any sort of stress, body and mind must be responsive. In an emergency, we must react quickly in an appropriate way, resisting or giving way as necessary. This instinctive feel for survival is the 'fight or flight' response of the adrenal glands just above the kidneys, which are responsible for preparing us for rapid action when faced with the threat of danger.

Like the adrenal glands, the base chakra has a relationship with the circulatory system and the blood supply. It also influences the skeletal muscles of the arms, legs and torso that allow us to move through the world. The base chakra is linked to the colour red and is responsible for maintaining the body's heat – the core temperature that allows chemical reactions to take place in the cells at the correct rate.

◁ Both the inability to sustain energy levels and the need for continual excitement or stimulation can indicate imbalance in the base chakra.

TO ENERGIZE THE BASE CHAKRA

Exercising the sense of touch, attending to practical matters, gentle movement and exercise can help to energize and re-connect us to the base chakra. Any of the following will help:

• A warm bath.

• Massage, aromatherapy or reflexology.

• Walking, running, jumping or stamping the feet improves the circulation, coordination and our link to the planet.

• Eating, especially high protein foods. Taking a good mineral supplement may also help. A shortage of zinc is one of the commonest causes of 'spaciness' and lack of mental focus.

▽ Any activity, such as bathing, that emphasizes physicality and stimulates the senses – especially smell – helps to balance the base chakra.

Imbalances in the base chakra can show up in many ways. Characteristic symptoms include a chronic lack of energy, with exhaustion following even slight exercise, problems with stiffness and painful movement, particularly in the hips, legs and feet. When poor physical coordination or poor circulation (a tendency to have cold hands and feet) is present, the base chakra is worth looking at.

The base chakra may also need healing and energizing when someone is uncomfortable with their body. This can lead to a sense of confusion or unreality and may show in a lack of drive or motivation and an aversion to getting involved in practicalities or physical exercise. Conversely, an imbalance in the base chakra can also cause excessive tension or excitability, with a continual need for stimulation.

Base chakra – seat of passion

The emotional responses that are associated with the base chakra express the need to ensure personal survival. They tend to be direct, explosive and strong, yet once satisfied, they will dissipate immediately. Young babies, in whom the base chakra is dominant, clearly demonstrate these qualities. They will express themselves forcefully and loudly whenever they are hungry, tired or uncomfortable, yet will fall asleep quickly once satisfied.

fear

Whenever there is a sense of loss of control or powerlessness, the base chakra energies and our survival instincts are activated. The fiery emotional states of anger, assertiveness and aggression all arise from one fundamental cause, and that is fear. Fear begins as soon as it seems that there is a loss of control, or a sense of being trapped. A dramatic response is still a biological necessity in some cases, but unfortunately as life has become more complicated, it is much less possible to feel that we are really in control of our own existence. Television, for example, presents us with events from all over the world over which we have no control, and yet we experience them emotionally and our bodies automatically

▽ The innate survival instincts of the base chakra automatically activate whenever we feel threatened or powerless.

respond as if we were actually involved. Our means for survival – food, water, heat, light and money – are all supplied to us by others. In these circumstances it is quite easy to become habitually fearful. This usually manifests itself as stress, which is an increasing inability to deal with changing situations in a flexible, creative way. Depending on the personality, stress and fear will show as either withdrawal – like a trapped animal hiding in a corner pretending not to be there – or aggression, in which case even those offering help will be perceived as a threat and attacked.

Remaining in a constant state of alert drains the body's energy and makes it more difficult to respond effectively when real danger presents itself. This can cause an emotional burn-out, which makes it impossible to become excited or motivated by anything.

▽ The physicality and immediacy of passion easily bypasses the rational mind. It is energy that must be expressed immediately.

releasing energies

There may be times when you feel the need to release an excess of base chakra emotional energy. There are several ways to do this. A simple and effective method, and a good way to begin, is to describe your strong feelings in writing, without judging them or censoring them. When you have finished writing your account, burn everything that you have written. This is the important element. The content of your writing is not important – it merely serves to let go of the excess energy.

When you are feeling the effects of withdrawal from emotional involvement, routine physical activities such as gardening, washing and cleaning can be helpful. Running, drumming, or dancing to music with a strong rhythm will keep the energy circulating and prevent a build-up.

It is a lot easier, however, to release an excess of base chakra energy, than it is to build it up if it is lacking. Poor motivation is one of the main features of insufficient energy in this chakra.

△ Strong feelings initiated by the base chakra should not be held on to. Writing the feelings on a piece of paper and then symbolically burning them in a fire can help to release them.

▽ Channelling strong feelings into a simple, constructive activity, however mundane, helps to take the pressure off and regulates the safety valve of the base chakra.

passion

Lust, physical passion and sexual excitement are complex emotions. They all involve many different chakras. But it is the motivation to ensure survival of the species that underlies immediate physical attraction, and this is associated with the base chakra. In this capacity the base chakra functions at many levels, promoting circulation, excitement, instinct and spontaneity and helping us to focus on the physical body in the present.

Imbalance within the base chakra can show as a build-up of strong emotions, which may then be released inappropriately or excessively. There can be a tendency to selfishness and a lack of concern for others, or a total denial of the emotions we are actually experiencing, especially anger. Lack of assertiveness can also indicate difficulties in this area.

Base chakra – the pioneer

The base chakra gives the energy and motivation needed to make good use of whatever resources are available. One of the main functions of the base chakra is to solidify, to make real. This includes the realization of dreams and the maintainance of energy levels within the body.

In order to survive, the human race learned to be very good at inventing and making new tools and creating new technologies. The base chakra is essential in the manifestation of any idea, dream or concept. Without its down-to-earth energy, it doesn't matter how wonderful our inspiration is or how useful a new invention may one day prove to be. The base chakra will find whatever is solid and viable in the most ephemeral concept and enable it to be made manifest and useful.

action

The desire to act, to move, to do, is an expression of the powerful energy of the base chakra. This energy is an absolute prerequisite for any new venture or project. Creativity, though, involves nearly every one of the main chakra centres in some way. Acting only by itself, the base chakra would be likely to 'make do' with the first thing it came up with and might well completely destroy it if it did not work right away.

Complete involvement in the practicality of making something new is a characteristic of this energy. The need is to see something coming into existence through personal skill

▽ Surviving in dangerous situations puts our attention on our physical skills, our sense and our feelings of being alive – all base chakra qualities.

△ Whatever the drive of the base chakra may be, without sufficient food to sustain the physical body, nothing will be achieved.

and effort. As soon as it is there, taking its place in the real world, the job of the first chakra is done, and unless supported by other energies, the creator will become quickly distracted by another new project.

This short-lived burst of energy can be useful in an appropriate context. For example, people with the dynamic skills associated with the base chakra are happy to create possibilities but content to let others work on the fine details. They are not interested in keeping total control, so allow space for others to follow in their work.

going boldly...

The base chakra energy is the pioneer, always willing to go where no one has gone before and to do things that have never been done. In a balanced base chakra there is the energy, confidence, know-how and dexterity to survive and thrive in the moment-to-moment exploration of new territory. Exploring, mountain climbing, white-water rafting, and all other activities where people voluntarily put themselves in a completely self-reliant situation, engage with the survival instincts of the base chakra.

When base chakra energy is excessively dominating, however, only experiences that are life-threatening are enjoyed, and only the making of new things is important, not the uses to which they are put; 'doing' becomes the only comfortable state and 'being' is intolerably boring. Such states may arise from habit patterns that develop when there is actually a significant underlying lack of security. People with this problem feel the need to keep busy, which is often an attempt to disguise a sense of emptiness, a huge void that seems to threaten the existence of the individual.

The energy of the base chakra is one of concentration and gravity, so a feeling of vacuum, completely free from solidity and form, unable to be held or defined in any

▽ Base chakra energy initiates new projects but by itself will soon become distracted. We need other chakras to support and sustain our enthusiasm through to completion.

SELF-PARENTING

This exercise helps to resolve some of the earliest memories and concepts we have around feelings of security and self-identity. It can help to release stresses held within the base chakra.
1 Settle yourself in a quiet, dimly lit room. In your imagination take yourself back to the moment of your conception. How would you like it to have been?
2 Move forward in time and see yourself as a baby in the womb, as a newborn child and as a young child. Imagine at each stage that you are happy, content, comfortable and as secure as you can be. Feel that sense of security throughout your body.
3 Sort out a daily routine that allows you more time to fulfil all your personal needs in every possible way. Try to follow that routine for a day, then a few days, then maybe a week. Allow the process to become a natural part of your routine, and feel the benefit of this self-parenting.

way at all, is completely alien to it. This feeling of emptiness often arises in situations where something established and apparently solid (a state the base chakra understands very well), becomes subject to change, death or decay. As change is the only constant in our lives, it is difficult for us to deal with the times when we feel our very foundations have been removed. Everyone will cope in different ways with such a situation, but it can be helpful to watch ourselves to ensure that our chakra energies, and the various activities they reflect, remain as evenly balanced as possible. Getting stuck in one chakra state will only lead to energy collapse sooner or later.

Base chakra imbalance at the mental level can show as obsessive focus on one thing to the exclusion of everything else, or else as a rigid and materialistic outlook that usually also masks deep insecurities about personal survival issues. People who are interested in only new and risky or dangerous ventures, or who show the opposite trait of being completely lacking in practicality, disintegrating into confusion when faced with practical projects or being unable to complete anything, might benefit from work with the base chakra.

Base chakra – the fortress

The spiritual purpose of the base chakra is the protection of individual integrity. The base holds together the fabric of the personality and is the very real foundation for every spiritual discipline. This energy centre is the place where the ladder to heaven rests. Unless that ground is completely solid in every respect, little else of true value will be accomplished.

anchor

The base chakra must be well balanced in order to anchor and make use of spiritual energy so that it can be of value to us here and now. The more someone works with spiritual growth and development, the more vital it becomes to anchor those energies. We are adrift in an ocean of different energies, physical, electromagnetic and subtle. Some are obvious to the senses, like those that create the weather. Others are more subtle, such as the electromagnetic fields that cover the planet from both natural and artigicial sources. Each of these energy fields has the potential to disrupt the way we function if it bombards us with a

▽ **Without the grounding influence of the base chakra our system would be constantly upset by the changing tides of energy around us.**

THE WARRIOR
This yoga posture stabilizes the base chakra. You may be surprised at how much heat this static posture generates. Remember to breathe normally while you are doing it.

1 Loosen your clothes and take off your shoes and socks. Spread your feet apart, to make a triangle of equal sides with the ground.

2 Stretch your arms out to the sides, and rotate your left foot outwards. Bend your left knee, keeping the right leg straight. When you reach a position where you could be sitting on an imaginary chair – stop.
3 Hold the pose for as long as is comfortable, then return to standing.
4 Repeat to the right, holding the pose for the same length of time.

vibration that is stronger than our own. This is the process called entrainment, where an energy with a strong coherent pattern begins to make weaker, more disorganized energy fields vibrate at its own frequency.

Taking the analogy from electricity a little further: if we do not have an effective way of earthing outside energies, static will build up and begin to interfere with our own 'signal'. The base chakra is that lightning rod, that earth cable, which prevents unwanted energy signals from destroying our equilibrium.

One indication to look for that suggests a spiritual imbalance in the base chakra is an 'otherworldliness', a loss of awareness and

▽ The solid form and orderliness of the mineral kingdom reflects the nature of the base chakra. Dark-coloured crystals naturally ground and centre our own energies.

△ The purpose of meditation is to let go of all excess activity in the mind, emotions and body in order to experience the world as it is – not to escape from reality.

▽ Dancing and drumming have been used for millennia as a means to attain spiritual states. Energizing the base chakra, and all other chakras in turn, strengthens the body and spirit.

interest in the real world and in practical survival issues. There may also be a lack of discipline, an unfocused attitude, wishful thinking and fantasizing or a dissociation from the body and its requirements, often accompanied by a desire to escape physical incarnation. People with a weak base chakra may be easily swayed by their impressions, lack the ability to discriminate between viewpoints and belief systems, or receive psychic and clairvoyant messages over which they have little or no control. A lack of grounding can create hyperactivity, restlessness, the inability to settle, and very volatile emotions.

Grounding and earthing restores the natural flow of energy to and from the base chakra, and visualization is helpful. With your feet firmly on the ground, imagine tree roots extending down and out from where you are touching the ground. With each outbreath imagine the roots growing deeper and more firmly into the earth. With each inbreath, allow the sustaining energy of the Earth to flow through your whole body.

Sacral chakra – the pleasure principle

34

the chakras of manifestation

The sacral chakra is the second energy centre. It is located in the area below the navel and above the pubic bone, at the front of the pelvis. Physically this chakra is involved with the organs of the lower abdomen – the large intestine, the bladder and the reproductive organs.

Detoxification is one of the key functions of the sacral chakra, at every level, from the physical through to the spiritual.

▷ **The sacral chakra is the reservoir of our life energy, from which energy, or chi, is chanelled or directed through the rest of the body.**

▽ **The sacral chakra, located in the area below the navel and above the pubic bone, is the second energy centre.**

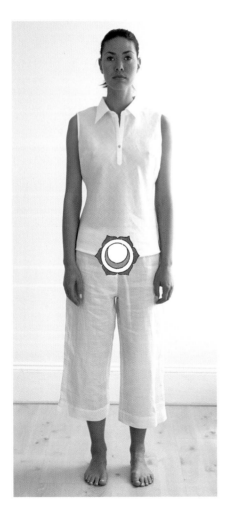

Traditionally this chakra is connected with the element of water and has its characteristics of flow, cleansing and movement. The symbol of the chakra is a white, blue or silver crescent, which is also a reminder of the moon's influence on all things watery, including the ebb and flow of the emotions.

So while the defining characteristic of the base chakra is the element of Earth, representing solidity, focus and the structure of the skeletal system, the sacral chakra represents the polar opposites of these: flow, flexibility and the emptiness or hollowness of the body's organs – bladder, intestine, womb and so on.

The whole pelvic region is shaped like a bowl, in which the energy focus of the sacral chakra lies. The pelvis is shaped to support the legs and the many different muscles that control their movement. Any strain or tension here can create a whole range of symptoms, from lower back pain, irregular or painful menstruation, constipation and sciatica to problems with fertility, impotence and fluid balance in the body.

Any disease state that features poor balance of fluids or flexibility will correspond to an imbalance within the second chakra. Water

▷ **Belly-dancing is an ideal activity to balance the sacral energies. It strengthens the pelvic and abdominal muscles and it encourages flexibility.**

△ **The sacral chakra is associated with the energy of the moon and with the emotions and fluids of the body.**

absorption is an important function of the large intestine, while control of the mineral and water balance in the blood is regulated by the kidneys. If the functions of these areas are impaired, the balance of chemicals in the body is upset, and it becomes more difficult to eliminate toxins and waste products, which effectively poison the body.

It is the job of the sacral chakra to keep things moving. Any rigidity of the joints, such as in arthritis and other similar conditions, can also reflect unbalanced energy at this centre.

balance and flow

The area of the sacral chakra within the pelvis is also our centre of gravity. It rules our sense of movement and balance, and gives grace and flow to our activity. It is the reservoir of what the Indians call prana and the Chinese call *chi* – the life-energy that infuses every living system, the subtle substance within the breath that is so important in the spiritual disciplines of the

WU CHI

One way of energizing and balancing the sacral chakra is to take up belly dancing. Another is to perform this standing posture exercise, called wu chi in Chinese. Begin by holding the posture for between two and five minutes, then increase the time gradually.

1 Stand with your feet apart, directly under your shoulders.

2 Let your hands hang loosely by your sides and allow your shoulders to drop.

3 Imagine your whole body is hanging by a thread attached to the top of your head, suspending you from the ceiling.

4 Allow yourself to relax, making sure your knees are not locked. Breathe normally.

Watch as you become aware of the tensions in your muscles and the internal chatter of your mind. Let them go.

△ The slow, graceful, physical movements of Tai Chi and Chi Kung stimulate the flow of *chi*, which is visualized as a subtle substance with a consistency and speed of flow similar to honey.

East and in the martial arts that developed among the elite monks of the Hindus, Buddhists and Taoists.

Today the West is familiar with the disciplined exercises of Tai Chi and Chi Kung. They have developed over thousands of years as an effective way to control and direct the flow of the subtle force of *chi* through the body and even beyond, into the environment. One of the main centres for gathering and distributing *chi* is known in Chinese as *tan tien*. It is equivalent, though not identical, to the sacral chakra. The same place is called the *hara* in Japanese, the centre of the life-force. From this reservoir *chi* can be channelled and directed through the rest of the body to maintain health and give great amounts of strength and endurance, or to open up states of awareness.

It is only from a flow outwards from ourselves that we can begin to explore and experience the world that is not us. Remaining centred and solid within the security of the base chakra, our awareness can reach beyond the immediate, stretching out a curious hand to things just beyond our grasp. Movement and curiosity is required. The grace and balance of the sacral chakra's smooth flow of energy helps us succeed. Here we begin to experience the energy of the world around us.

Sacral chakra – feeling the need

The emotional level of the second chakra is reflected in its watery nature. Its activity is focused on flow, movement and exploration of the surroundings. Its motivation is enjoyment and pleasure and its reward is sensation – the invigoration of the senses.

The whole of life at the earliest stage of development revolves around feeling secure and well-fed. This is the level of the base chakra: making sure that survival is assured. Once these primary needs have been met, the priority is to explore the potential of the body through play, and to explore the surroundings using all the senses. This is where the sacral chakra comes in – any young animal playing is behaving under the influence of this chakra.

brain works

Experiments carried out to map activity in the brain show clearly that the first nerve pathways to be established directly after birth feed the parts of the brain where pleasure is registered. This helps the learning process of the infant, because it reinforces actions

△ Spontaneous enjoyment of experience, exploration of the senses and play are all characteristics of the sacral chakra, stimulating our ability to learn and develop as individuals.

that are more likely to be beneficial, rather than those that are more likely to cause damage, pain or suffering.

The parts of the brain concerned with registering pleasure – called the limbic system – also directly affect the hypothalamus. This small organ deep in the centre of the brain controls the hormone system and the activity of the autonomic nervous system – the involuntary processes that maintain balance in the heart rate, breathing and blood pressure.

enjoyment

Happiness and enjoyment are important factors in maintaining the smooth running of the individual. They have been built into our awareness to encourage us to stay in harmony with ourselves and the environment. The sacral chakra maintains

▽ In the animal world there is no distinction between playing and learning. Play leads to the development of skills for survival and a more successful life.

BADDHA KONASANA

Hatha yoga helps the flow of life energy and increases physical flexibility and resilience. This exercise, baddha konasana or the cobbler's pose, encourages energy flow in all levels of the sacral chakra.

1 Sit on the floor, bending your knees and keeping your back straight.
2 Turn the soles of your feet to face each other.
3 Place the fingers of both hands over your toes.
4 Allowing your knees to fall outwards, draw your feet in towards your body. Don't try to force your knees nearer the floor. The more you relax your pelvis, the more the muscles will allow the knees to fall.
5 Stay in this position for a few moments before relaxing.

this flow of communication between body and mind through sensation and emotion. In order to be most effective, the mind has to be aware of subtle changes in the feelings. Very often vague intuitions and 'gut' feelings are dismissed by the conscious mind because they are not precise enough. It is possible to educate the conscious mind to take notice of the flow of feelings and the energy fluctuations of the sacral centre, making us much more sensitive and responsive to what is going on around us.

Flowing in harmony with our own energy and with our surroundings requires a level of flexibility as well as the ability to change focus – to let go, when necessary, of things that are no longer useful or helpful to us. An imbalance in the sacral chakra often arises when for one reason or another

we become fixated on something that we refuse to admit to ourselves is actually inappropriate or unrealistic.

Indications that the sacral chakra is out of balance can be emotional over-sensitivity or an unhealthy emotional dependency on someone else. Very often this includes intrusive behaviour and a failure to respect normal boundaries. At the opposite extreme there may be rigidity, with a lack of physical or emotional flexibility. Repression of feelings, a fear of sensuality, sex, pleasure or enjoyment, as well as guilt over feelings and desires, all indicate sacral imbalance that can result in frustration and bitterness.

▷ **Adults who display sacral chakra imbalances may well have experienced a lack of close physical contact as young children.**

Sacral chakra – the artist within

The sacral chakra is located right in the centre of the womb area. It is thus related to fertility, giving birth and all other aspects of creativity. Creativity at the sacral chakra level is to do with manipulation of the senses and the world. At the orange level of the second chakra the process is very personal. It is a spontaneous mechanism to keep energy moving, to avoid the build-up of stress. The complementary blue chakra, the throat, is also related to the creative process but as a means of external expression, a way of communicating.

the nature of stress

Stress is commonly understood to be the accumulation of difficult and negative circumstances. In fact it is any stimulus, good or bad, enjoyable or painful, that throws the body out of balance to such a degree that it is unable fully to return to its previous equilibrium. It is a widely held belief that creativity can be stimulated by stress, and that true art therefore requires suffering. This is really a misunderstanding of the processes that are controlled and directed by the sacral chakra.

The accumulation of physical stress in the muscles and organs of the body, and emotional and mental stress in the subtle

▽ The flow of the emotions is experienced like the tides of the sea, changing from hour to hour. Any activity, such as making music, can quickly alter emotional states.

△ It is the activity of a creative act that is important in stimulating life-energy, not the quality or permanence of the end product.

bodies and chakras, creates a breakdown in the natural movement and flow of life-energy. This rigidity, if allowed to build up unchecked, leads to atrophy and eventually to death. Old age can be seen simply as this process of accumulating stress. Indeed old age is a relative term – some people who have hard, unforgiving lives look old at forty, while others, who are flexible and happy despite the hardships they have endured, look radiant at eighty.

Stress initiates survival drives, which are first chakra functions. But the trouble with stress is that if it is not dissipated quickly by 'fight or flight' responses, a different approach is needed. The more creative, flexible energy needed to give the right response is provided by the second chakra.

△ **Creative activity explores the flow of mind, body and spirit as they focus on one object. Successful art communicates this life-energy whatever the technical skills of the creator.**

flowing energy

Life-energy is like a stream, it must keep moving. Once it stops moving, a stream is no longer a stream. Likewise, life-energy that is blocked stops being life-giving. The sacral chakra helps to ensure the supply of life-energy available to us by keeping the flow in motion. Where stress creates blocks and rigidity the sacral chakra creates opportunities for life-energy to move around them, much as a stream will divert its flow to move around a build-up of debris in its path. Creative activity is like this diverted stream of energy, restoring the quality of flow back into the systems of the body.

The sacral chakra often initiates creative activity as a way of finding new solutions to intractable problems. This is a sense-based process of feeling the way to solutions, rather than a conscious, rational assessment and analysis of the situation. The process can begin when stress levels are high enough to stop normal activity. There is an impasse and at that still, quiet moment, some small unconscious act, such as doodling, grabs all the attention and focuses the flow of life-energy into the creative process. Depression and despair may sometimes precede creativity, but once begun, the process of release is like an increased force of water, strong enough to wash the accumulated debris of stress aside, restoring a natural flow of life-energy.

Creativity is the natural state of life-energy and it restores life to a natural balance. Successful art, beautiful design and skilful craftsmanship are exhilarating and life-supporting because they embody this flow of life-energy. Creativity should never be seen as the domain of the expert and the specialist. We all have a sacral chakra, which is the womb of creativity, within us. If we let its energy flow naturally, everything we do will be an expression of the joyful creativity of living.

Sacral chakra – healing the wounds

The sacral chakra is the focus of our experience of pleasure and also the first place that experiences any kind of pain. Wherever trauma and pain may be in the body, they are registered in the second chakra. Pain is also held there if the trauma the pain creates is not released. Any shock to the system breaks the usual flow of our

▽ The effects of an accident or shock can last well beyond the actual event, colouring our lives for many years.

life. For example, the memory of an accident often gets stuck in the mind, where it is relived continually.

The sacral chakra is primarily affected for two reasons. First, the life-energy or *chi* is tightly gathered in this area of the body, so any threat to it causes turbulence and upset here. Second, it is the function of the sacral chakra to maintain the flow of life, which helps to remove the fragments of trauma locked within the different systems of the body.

EMOTIONAL STRESS RELEASE (ESR)
One of the most effective ways to release stress is lightly to touch the frontal eminences of the skull. These are two slight bumps above the outer edge of the eye at either side of the forehead. While stress is being released a slight irregular pulsing can often be felt at the eminences, which dies away once the process is complete.

1 Lightly hold the fingertips to the frontal eminences of the skull, or hold a hand across the forehead to catch both points easily.
2 Turning your attention to the stressful event will now automatically begin to release the accumulated tensions. It is not necessary to relive each event in detail, though often this occurs automatically. Strong feeling and emotions, as well as physical reaction, may surface while these points are being held.
3 As long as the process is allowed to complete itself, the body quickly and effectively releases the frozen memories once and for all.

▷ Stress becomes physically locked into the body as well as into the chakras. Intellectual understanding of a trauma alone is not always enough to remove it.

shock release

Emotional and mental shock can heal like broken bones, but scars may last for a long time, subtly affecting how we think and feel. Each event distorts or locks away energy that we need for our everyday lives. It takes a lot of psychic energy to separate memories of pain from our awareness and, like unwanted baggage, they load us down.

There are some very effective ways to help the sacral chakra release and let go of trauma and shock without the need to go through the pain of reliving the event. Counselling methods and psychological examination of trauma have been shown sometimes to increase, not decrease, stress levels. This is because the practical release of stress is a priority of the body, not simply an intellectual understanding of how the stress has been affecting behaviour. The sites, such as the sacral chakra, where the actual stress is located, need to be re-integrated into the present before the imbalances can be released effectively. One way to do this is to try the Emotional Stress Release exercise on the opposite page. It is important to remember that memories, particularly painful ones, tend to be stored with other memories that are in some way related. Releasing stress that initially appears to be caused by a minor event may be an opportunity for the body to let go of many other stresses that deal with a similar scenario or emotion.

An upset digestive system, particularly constipation, can indicate that stress and trauma are interfering with normal functioning. There may be an inability to become emotionally involved with life and to enjoy it. Emotional volatility and a tendency to aggressive behaviour or tearfulness at the slightest provocation are other signs of problems. Inability to let go of a stressful event, so that it preys on the mind, shows that this chakra is blocked, as does suffering from an increasing number of infections and illnesses.

CRYSTAL RELEASE
The sacral chakra can be supported in its release of stress by using a particular layout of crystals. You will need three clear quartz crystals, together with three moonstones or three rose quartz crystals.

1 With the three clear quartz crystals make a downward pointing triangle below the navel. If the crystals have points, these should point outwards.
2 Below these crystals and above the pubic bone, make an arc of the three remaining stones.

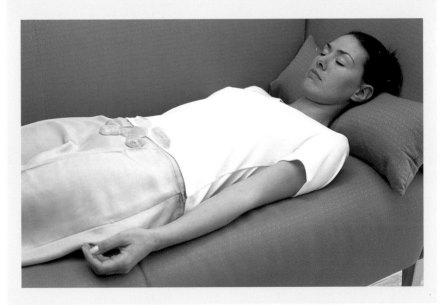

The Chakras of Relationship

The third and fourth chakras are at the solar plexus and the heart. They begin to integrate our energy with the environment and the people around us. Growth always involves expanding into new areas, so the skills of recognizing potential dangers and establishing a place of personal power are essential.

Solar plexus chakra – the organizer

The solar plexus, the third centre, is considered as a single chakra, but is, as the word 'plexus' suggests, a fusion of many different energies. Midway between the ribcage and the navel, it also corresponds to the lumbar vertebrae in the spine. The physical attributes of the solar plexus chakra fall into three main areas: the digestion, the nervous system and the immune system.

digestion

The process of digestion and assimilation of nutrients is vital to sustain life. The organs linked to the solar plexus are the stomach,

▽ The solar plexus chakra, below the ribcage, is the main organizing principle affecting all parts of the body and mind.

△ The solar plexus chakra is associated with the element of Fire, not only because it creates physical heat in the body, but also because it takes raw materials and transforms them.

▽ The solar plexus chakra is often referred to as the fusebox of the body. In this area are large concentrations of nerve tissue that, if disrupted, can affect the whole nervous system.

liver, gallbladder, pancreas, duodenum and small intestine. For digestion and the assimilation of nutrients to be successful, all these organs have to work in harmony. This involves a series of chemical reactions using a great many different catalysts. From the alkaline enzyme-rich saliva in the mouth, food moves to the acidity of the stomach. Here it is churned, thoroughly mixing the natural acids and enzymes. It then passes into the duodenum, where bile from the liver, via the gallbladder, begins to break down fats, and more enzymes from the pancreas begin to act on sugars and carbohydrates. As the mixture moves through the small intestine, the valuable nutrients from the food are absorbed through the wall of the intestine into the bloodstream. Failure to digest food efficiently means that nutrients are not absorbed.

immune system

The immune system works like a library or a computer. It stores and categorizes information about everything the body encounters. For instance, on meeting a virus, the body recognizes it as an enemy and activates the defence mechanisms to fight and overcome the infection. If the body later encounters the same virus again it has the information to prevent a serious invasion.

Problems with this identification process often show up when the body reacts to harmless or even beneficial substances as if they are dangerous. This is experienced as allergy or intolerance. The opposite malfunction happens when the body harbours an infection for a long time because it fails to recognize its presence and

so neglects to fight it at all. Difficulties also occur when the body fails to recognize its own enzymes, hormones or neuro-transmitters, and sometimes there is an inability to recognize minerals and vitamins that should be absorbed by the small intestine. These problems surface as deficiencies but do not respond to increased intake because the problem is not lack, but a failure to recognize the substance.

The solar plexus chakra is put under great pressure by the way we live today. Its physical functions are strained by the types of food we eat, the pace of life and new toxins in our environment. It is not surprising that many of the diseases in our society today are a sign of some dysfunction in the solar plexus chakra.

ARDHA MATSEYANDRASANA

This exercise, the spinal twist, tones the whole of the solar plexus. The more upright you keep your spine, the easier it is to twist.

1 Kneel down on a blanket or thick mat, resting on your heels. Slide your buttocks to the right of your feet. Lift your left leg, so the left foot is across the right knee.

2 Shuffle your bottom around to get comfortable and to keep your spine straight. Bring your left arm round behind you, resting your fingers on the floor to steady yourself. Bring your right arm to rest on the outside of the left leg, the elbow bracing against the knee. Breathe in, then as you breathe out, lift your spine and twist round to look over your left shoulder. Breathe normally.

3 When you feel ready to release the pose, breathe in, then as you breathe out, unwind yourself. First bring your left arm back around to the front and follow its movement with the head, naturally straightening the spine. If you are unable to stretch into the full twist, simply hold the knee instead of bracing it with an elbow. Repeat on the other side, mirroring the steps.

Solar plexus chakra – sun of contentment

The solar plexus chakra is often identified with the element of Fire. Our emotional reaction to fire is two-fold. Fire gives warmth and comfort but brings fear and terror when it gets out of control. This echoes the emotional breadth of the solar plexus chakra.

△ **The unknown cannot be controlled because there is a lack of information.** The mind becomes anxious and fearful.

fear

The key negative emotion that spawns all others is fear. It can become an underlying emotion that drives other everyday emotional reactions. Fear arises in any situation where the outcome seems beyond the capacity of the mind to determine, and there is an inability simply to relax. The mind conjures up limitless scenarios and gets locked into self-defeating thought processes of 'what if…'

Fear can escalate into terror or subside into anxiety in any area of life. Issues

◁ **Threats and rules that restrict our natural exuberance easily block the solar plexus chakra.**

VISUALIZING THE SUN

Use this visualization exercise to invite warmth and joy into your life. This is a good exercise to do if you have feelings of unease or fear that you want to dispel. Using the positive aspects and strength of the sun you will create a feeling of security and contentment.

1 Sit or lie down comfortably. Wrap a blanket around you if the day is cool. Breathe in, and as you breathe out, allow yourself to relax. Imagine a sphere of golden light beginning to form between your navel and the bottom of your ribcage. Imagine this sphere is also giving off a comfortable warmth. Allow the sphere to grow until it enfolds the whole of your body.
2 Stay still for a few minutes, allowing the light and warmth to fill every part of your body. Imagine the sphere shrinking back until it is the size of a tennis ball. Allow the small sphere to sink into your abdomen, before shrinking down to the size of a pea. Let the imagery dissolve. Bring your attention back to everyday awareness.

◁ When the solar plexus chakra is functioning well, we are able to accept happiness in our lives. We can feel and appreciate joy in the simplest of situations.

shame for this lack of compliance. Shame prevents us from working with the solar plexus chakra at the emotional level, and this drives us into interacting with the world primarily through our thoughts.

healing

In this area, healing can be approached in several ways. Allowing things to be as they are, rather than trying to control events, helps to remove fears. Expressing the Fire energy as anger helps to link the solar plexus with the sacral and base chakras.

People who experience a lot of anger often live so much in their minds that they do not realize how angry they are, especially with regard to authority figures who have dominated and disempowered them. Shame can often be recognized in internal conversations that replay critical comments from the past. Here the mental criticism, which effectively acts in the same way as a curse, needs to be neutralized by formulating an imaginary response from an adult standpoint.

concerning personal power are part of the solar plexus function. As children we were subject to the guidance of our parents, relatives and teachers, all of whom we related to and possibly still relate to, as figures of authority. If people in authority use their dominant position to force us into habit patterns that take our personal power from us, the solar plexus chakra becomes effectively blocked. Failure to accede to this dominance is often met by criticism and punishment. Subsequently we may feel

◁ The shame that might be felt from past humiliation by an authority figure can be neutralized in the present by visualizing the situation, changing the balance of power, and bringing the authority figure down to his or her proper size.

Solar plexus chakra – the librarian

Working at the mental level, the solar plexus chakra is one of the most powerful tools we have at our disposal to create our personal circumstances – our own heaven or hell. Sages and philosophers have known for thousands of years that personal belief systems, the thoughts by which we recognize and understand how the world appears to work, are of critical importance to our wellbeing.

recording

Like a librarian or custodian, this part of our 'body-mind' catalogues and files away experiences and information for reference and retrieval when it is required. To carry out this organizational task efficiently it is necessary to be able to identify things clearly and accurately, to label them correctly, to file them in the right place and to cross-index where necessary.

Failure to store information properly results in many difficulties. Confusion and fear often arise from false identification.

△ Memory has been shown to be a function of the whole brain (rather than specific areas). In order to retrieve memories, communication within the brain needs to be efficient.

Incorrect filing also creates confusion, learning problems and difficulties in retrieval (remembering). Inability to introduce cross-referencing severely limits the ability to integrate experiences.

If we are forced into certain learning situations before the solar plexus chakra, our personal librarian, is mature enough to cope, blocks occur around the issues involved and we develop negative belief systems about them. These beliefs will affect the way in which we interact with the world around us and create disharmony in that

◁ Concentration, analysis and effective study all rely on the balanced functioning of the solar plexus chakra.

MEMORY GAME

This game has many variations in different cultures. It exercises all aspects of the solar plexus chakra at the mental level – recognition, identification, categorization, recording and recall. This exercise can be repeated, preferably using different items. If you reach 25+ items you are doing very well. It is important that even if you can remember only five or so items, you do not get annoyed or disappointed with yourself. Practice improves scores. It is up to you how honest you are with yourself when doing this exercise.

1 Find around 30 small items and place them on a plain background. Cover the items with a cloth.

2 Collect a pen and paper. Uncover the items and look at them for not more than three minutes.

3 Cover the items with the cloth again. Write down as many items as you can remember.

relationship. Stresses build up and unless action is taken to correct the inaccurate beliefs, it usually results in physical, emotional and mental difficulties linked to the solar plexus chakra. If we are unable to identify events clearly, our capacity to judge, weigh up alternatives and make decisions becomes very limited.

◁ **The solar plexus chakra controls our ability to identify problems and find solutions to unlock our understanding.**

learning

In any learning situation, the information that needs to be learned has to be identified as such so that it can subsequently be catalogued correctly. Inability to learn or study may be the result of forced or inappropriate learning situations in early life. Stresses once created here will be remembered by the body-mind every time a similar situation arises. If the stress around the events can be released, new learning strategies can emerge.

Solar plexus chakra – know thyself

The solar plexus chakra at the spiritual level applies its energies to defining the boundaries of the self – the individual. The challenge at this level is to gain wisdom and insight into the true nature of the self beyond the everyday level of the persona.

It is not possible to define who you are unless you can also identify who and what you are not. Here the discrimination and judgment of the mental level of the solar plexus is brought to bear on the inner self. When you know who you are, you can start to understand your place in the world.

When we shine the clear light of understanding on ourselves, the first thing we tend to notice is faults and problems that have apparently been created in us by others. But as we look more closely, the need to blame others for the predicament in which we find ourselves recedes. We begin to realize that the only way forward is to transform the way we judge ourselves

△ It is necessary to turn our attention away from outer stimuli if we are to see ourselves clearly.

and others. A major sign of progress along the path to wisdom is accepting that the world owes you nothing and that you are no more important than anything else.

Solar plexus issues often arise from how we perceive ourselves in terms of our personal power. If, through experiences with overbearing authority figures, we have been led to believe that we are clumsy, stupid, worthless or bad, our whole relationship to the world will reflect this. We will feel powerless and prone to failure because of our perceived 'faults'. Similarly, if we come to believe that we are superior to other people, our actions will reflect this and there will be a tendency to ignore the wisdom of

◁ In nearly all spiritual philosophies the wisdom of the Self has been compared to the light of the sun. The perfect clarity of the solar plexus chakra clearly illuminates everything for what it is.

others and forget our own shortcomings or failures. In both situations, current events or circumstances might be identical but the powerless focus on failure, while the powerful focus on success.

Looking with the spiritual discrimination of the solar plexus chakra, both of these viewpoints have been created by incomplete information. Our own interpretation of reality is coloured by other people's eyes, minds and emotions. It is the job of the solar plexus chakra to realize at a spiritual level that all such judgments are limited and ultimately false. Our view of ourselves and others is no more substantial than clothing or masks.

Solar plexus energy can best be employed as power to do something, but very often slides into power over others. This turns into a competitive race, where we try in all sorts of ways to be better than others – more wealthy, more intelligent, more happy, more spiritual. If the energies have been distorted by bad experiences, we become more hard-done-by, more lonely and so on.

Allowing the solar plexus an opportunity to shine with the clarity of the sun encourages a broader perspective where these false judgments can begin to be seen as the ephemeral shadows they really are.

▽ **Embrace and accept yourself in the same way as you love and appreciate your closest friends.**

MEDITATION WITHOUT FORM

This is one of the easiest, though some say also the hardest, ways of beginning to perceive the boundaries between your everyday self and the finer levels of your whole being. It is sometimes called meditation without form, and uses only the breath as a focus. Because you are always in the present during this exercise, if there is a sudden noise you should not be startled at all. But if you have disappeared into your thoughts or imaginings, away from the attention on your breath, you will find external noises quite disruptive. Begin by doing this for five minutes. As you become more practised, gradually extend the time to 20 minutes.

Sit in a comfortable position, upright but relaxed. Place your hands in your lap, the right resting on the left. Close your eyes partially, so that light still enters but no clear image can be seen. Leave your mouth slightly open and rest the tip of your tongue on the roof of your mouth, just behind your teeth. Turn your attention to the movement of your breath as it enters and leaves your body. Don't think about your breath, or try to control it, just keep your attention on it. When you become aware that your mind has wandered and you have been thinking about something else, gently bring your attention back to your breath and continue.

Heart chakra – embracing the world

The heart chakra is located near the centre of the breastbone or sternum. The physical organs and parts of the body linked to this chakra are characterized by their actions of expansion and contraction, drawing in and pushing away.

physical attributes

The heart, with its rhythmic expansion and contraction, is the powerful muscular pump that sends oxygenated blood to all parts of the body. By its movement, the diaphragm, the powerful muscle below the lungs, creates changes in pressure, allowing us to breathe in fresh air. As the diaphragm contracts, the

▽ The heart chakra is at the centre of the main chakras and is the balance point for the system.

△ The heart chakra governs our interactions as we reach out to touch and embrace other people.

outbreath expels carbon dioxide from the body. The lungs are composed of tree-like air ducts that bring air into contact with the bloodstream. The blood picks up oxygen from the air, releasing back into it carbon dioxide and other waste products as it returns from its journey through the body.

These processes of expansion, interchange and contraction are reflected in our relationship with the world. The heart chakra regulates our interaction, making sure that we become neither too involved nor too remote from the world around us. The relationship is in constant motion: if it stays stationary all balance is lost. Reaching out and physically touching helps us to gather information. As we gather information we respond and begin to relate.

The action of the arms can be one of enfolding, enclosing, embracing and absorption. Equally, the arms can defend, push away and protect. The degree to which we keep the physical balance between what

is outside us and our inner being is often reflected in the way we hold our upper torso and arms. Tension and rigidity suggest stasis and defensiveness. A relaxed stance and flowing movement not only shows ease with the world, it reduces the stress levels on the heart and lungs.

▽ Arms and hands are the executors of the heart chakra energy. They reach out to hold or ward off the world around us.

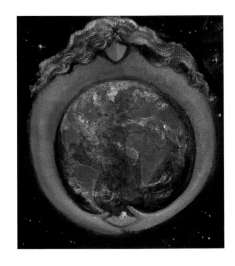

GOMUKHASANA

This exercise extends the muscles and cavities of the chest and stretches and energizes the shoulders and arms. If your hands do not meet, hold a piece of cane or wood 25–30 cm (10–12 in) to link your hands instead.

1 Kneel on a blanket or mat, sitting back on your heels. Stretch both arms out in front of you.

2 Raise your left arm over your head, bending it at the elbow so the left hand rests near the top of your back.
3 Sweep your right arm round to the right side, bending it at the elbow, sending the right hand up your back.
4 If your hands meet, lightly clasp your fingers, otherwise hold each end of the piece of wood.

5 When you have a grip on your hands, or the wood, take a breath in and bring your hands closer together, expanding your chest. Breathe normally. On an outbreath, loosen your grip then repeat, starting by raising your right hand above your head and mirroring the above stages.

Heart chakra   touching others

The art of balance is a theme that runs through all levels of the heart chakra. The element associated with this chakra is Air. Air flows from areas of high pressure towards areas of low pressure, always seeking a state of equilibrium. Likewise, the heart chakra continually strives to bring balance between external stimuli and internal emotions.

love

The experience of love is characterized by the flow of emotion. Falling in love is a wonderful, scary experience, but for every falling in love there is a falling out of love. Unless we accept this natural balancing mechanism, falling in love can become a fearful experience because of the inevitable grief and abandonment that accompanies falling out of love again. Understanding that ebb and flow happens from day to day, from moment to moment, eases any temporary sense of loss. Trying to hold on to any fluid emotional state like love will lead to an obsessive, possessive attachment reminiscent of an imbalanced sacral chakra response, or that of a four- to seven-year-old child.

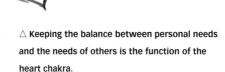

△ **Keeping the balance between personal needs and the needs of others is the function of the heart chakra.**

acceptance

A balanced and coherent heart chakra is shown in the ability to accept ourselves, other people and all sorts of situations. Without a real self-acceptance there is no

▽ **The importance of unconditional love is never greater than in a parent-child relationship.**

way that we are able to tolerate the foibles and faults of others. When we feel comfortable in ourselves, with all our faults, we are less likely to be insecure or threatened by those who, through their own envy, jealousy or lack of self-worth, try to dominate or control everything and everyone around them.

relationships

Any relationship can be heaven or hell. In a balanced relationship, each person has autonomy, but both also share. In relationships that are unhealthy, love is conditional to the point of being a weapon used to coerce the other into behaving or responding as required. Phrases like 'Well, if you really loved me you would…' and 'I'm doing this because I think it's good for you and I love you…' make a relationship one-sided. Many of us experience this threatened withdrawal of love as small children, and until our heart chakras become truly balanced, we may continue to play out the same pattern on our own children, family and friends.

BALANCING A RELATIONSHIP

This visualization exercise can be helpful in sorting out a difficult relationship, or in finding solutions to problems in relationships where one partner shows an unhealthy dependence on the other. It encourages a personal sense of space and helps you to reach an acknowledgement of the qualities of the other person. You can repeat the exercise as often as you feel it is necessary.

1 Set aside some quiet time when you are unlikely to be disturbed. Sit in a comfortable position, in a chair or on the floor, with an empty cushion or chair placed near you. Close your eyes, breathing slowly and calmly, and settle yourself.

2 Once your breathing has slowed and you are feeling calm, start to visualize a cylinder of gold light shining all around you, reaching down into the ground and rising up above your head.

3 On the other cushion, or in the empty chair, visualize the person with whom you have a relationship that needs to be rebalanced.

4 As you visualize the person sitting near you, recognize the qualities in them that you feel are causing difficulties between you in your relationship. Recognize, also, all the qualities in them that you appreciate or admire.

5 Visualize a second cylinder of gold light surrounding the other person. In your mind's eye, visualize both of you sitting within your own separate cylinders of gold light. If you notice any stray threads of light connecting the two cylinders, allow them to dissolve. Become aware of the space between you and the other person. Slowly return to normal awareness.

Heart chakra – freedom to be

Most people are aware that their physical appearance and attributes are inherited through their genes from each parent. It is not so well recognized that we also inherit many of our thinking patterns in the same way.

inheritance

Dominant beliefs, especially negative ones, can be traced through several successive generations. If we remain tied to these beliefs we never discover who we are and independence is never really achieved.

Following the rules drawn up by someone else gives us guidelines and lists of what we 'should' or 'ought' to do in order to develop a sense of duty and responsibility. These rules may have been enforced in some way, to mould us into the person the maker of the rules had in mind. This process can create, for the most part, a very harmonious society in which to live.

In some work situations, especially those dealing with emergency services, following the rules becomes a survival issue. While everyday life does not have that sort of intensity, for some people 'following the rules' remains an absolute necessity. This type of thinking has a robotic quality, producing people whose interaction can only follow a set formula or etiquette.

values

As the heart chakra matures, the individual starts to examine the rules to see whether they are really valid. Repression and restriction becomes intolerable. Outright rebellion may seem to be the only way to break free of the suffocating pattern. Society as a whole does not deal kindly with people

◁ In modern urban society the individual is moulded to fit in with a required role. Personal freedom may be exchanged for rigid order.

who question the consensus: this stage of individualization can thus be a lonely journey. The best outcome is the development of a personal set of values and ethics by which to live, which may be based on the old rules, but come from a fresh, up-to-date perspective with a personal relevance. It has been said by philosophers that there is no freedom without discipline. When a balanced state of individual self-discipline is achieved, self-acceptance and freedom become possible.

In many cultures, such as classical India and China, it was accepted that at some stage of life a removal from the rigidity of normal society was a natural phase of personal development. Usually this occurred in later life, when family responsibilities were no longer an issue. Individuals could concentrate on spiritual disciplines or remove themselves to remote spots to perfect skills of poetry or painting. In most cases, the rebellious can find alternative societies where they feel free from control, although every group imposes its own rules and taboos, which offer the kind of orderly balance the individual needs. This clearly demonstrates that restrictions are a burden only when they do not offer a balance to the unique heart chakra needs of each of us.

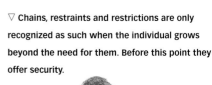

△ Expansion, growth and freedom are all pre-requisites for a healthy and mature heart chakra.

Whatever the rules and regulations of a society may be, those who are openly rebellious become primary targets for the criticism of the group. Today's behaviour censors are the tabloid press, who rely on the unusual behaviour of individuals to sustain their demand for interesting stories. At the same time, the media tend to take a tribal stance, rejecting new concepts and unique insights in favour of the establishment viewpoint. There are always, though, small groups and individuals on the edge of society who are prepared to explore new balances and create new patterns.

▽ Chains, restraints and restrictions are only recognized as such when the individual grows beyond the need for them. Before this point they offer security.

INDIVIDUAL OR INHERITED BELIEFS?

If you want or need to begin to de-programme yourself from values that are not yours, this exercise may help.

1 Take time to think about, then list on a sheet of paper, beliefs that begin with 'I should...' Add to your list over a period of a week or so, then don't look at it for a week. Look at the list – seeing if you can identify any of the statements with older family members, teachers or partners. If you do notice any links, ask yourself if you honestly believe the statement. Reflect on the relevance of the other statements you have made to your present life. Cross out those that no longer apply.

2 Copy out a list of the remaining statements, then leave them for another week. Repeat the self-questioning process. If there are any statements left on the list, they may highlight key issues that need dealing with or healing. They could also show you some of your present key values.

3 A similar exercise focuses on your wishes. Make a list beginning 'I want...' Be completely honest and open with yourself. This has nothing to do with judging what is good or bad. Neither should you exclude things that seem to be unlikely, impossible or silly. Acknowledging your drives and ambitions, your daydreams and fantasies in this way can release many hidden levels of stress from your heart chakra and may allow your conscious awareness to move in a direction that is more self-fulfilling.

Heart chakra – following the heart

At a certain point in the development and maturing of the heart chakra there is an opportunity to see yourself and the rest of the world from a very different perspective. This new view of the world can present some discomfort if the inherent patterning has always been to look outside yourself for confirmation and verification of your own worth. The realization dawns that while you can care, love and share with others you cannot live their lives for them or live your life through them. It can also be a very lonely moment when you realize that others cannot live your life for you either. They can love you, advise you and commiserate with you, but in the end, everyone is responsible only for themselves. Everybody has their unique direction in life.

△ The heart chakra allows us to expand and grow in power while keeping harmony with the Earth and everything around us.

BALANCING THE INNER AND OUTER WORLDS

This exercise helps to balance your relationship with the world and can be extremely calming. Sit or lie down in a comfortable position.

1 Breathe in then, as you breathe out, allow your body to relax. Visualize a flower giving off light at your heart chakra. Stay with that flower for a minute or two, feeling its energy and presence. In the centre of that flower, visualize the whole Earth.

Imagine the light of the flower filling the whole planet with incredible joy. Allow that joy and light to fill all of you too. Let that energy reach every single part of you, clearing away all negativity.

2 After a few minutes, bring your hands together over the heart chakra in the centre of your chest. Feel the energy under your hands and allow your hands to release that energy by slowly returning them to their original position lying in your lap.

Visualize the Earth at the centre of the flower at your heart chakra, melting into the flower and then the flower melting into your heart. Stay with this thought for a moment before slowly returning to normal awareness.

balance

If we are able to accommodate the paradoxical themes of the heart chakra, we can follow our own path while allowing others to follow theirs. The saying: 'If you love somebody, set them free' encapsulates the energy of a fully functional heart chakra. No matter how much you have shared with, taught, sacrificed for and loved someone, letting them be themselves is the greatest gift you can give. This releasing of the other person allows any possessiveness, misplaced sense of responsibility or dependence to disappear, and enables both of you to grow.

compassion

When you are able to achieve some sort of balance between yourself and everything outside yourself, the way opens for a special mix of compassion and caring. With this balance comes the understanding that, although the boundaries between the self and the world needed to be clear to get to this point, when you arrive there are no boundaries. This is not a sacrificial relationship with the world, but a complete openness and acceptance of it. In order to progress as a spiritual human being, avoiding

▷ At its spiritual level of function the heart chakra directs us along our path of life in a way that allows us to achieve our maximum potential.

the pitfalls of spiritual self-deception and egotism, it is necessary to arrive at a real awareness that, because all creation is connected, you cannot truly be free until everything else is too. The open acceptance of the world, and the awareness that the individual's spiritual development benefits everything, everywhere, is known as 'bodhicitta' or 'complete openness of mind'.

Bodhicitta has been fully explored in Buddhist traditions. It is found in the simple awareness of offering kindness to others at every possible opportunity. The Buddhist cosmology is huge, with millions of universes existing for millions of aeons. Within this ungraspable vastness of space and time, individuals are said to have incarnated numberless times. If this is the case then everyone we meet and every being we come across has, at one time or another, been our mother and has looked after, loved and cared for us to the best of their ability. In this context bodhicitta is simply acknowledging these past kindnesses.

▽ Equilibrium, or balance is the key to the heart chakra energy. Without it there can be no way for us to adapt to constant change.

The Chakras of Communication

The upper three chakras are at the base of the throat, the centre of the forehead and just above the crown of the head. They are physically close together and regulate our communication with and understanding of the world. The throat chakra focuses on the expression of what we know and feel. The brow chakra brings clarity of perception and intuitive insight, and the crown chakra unites the individual to the greater universe.

Throat chakra – finding peace

Blue is the colour associated with the throat chakra. It is the colour of communication and information but is also the colour of peacefulness. The human nervous system is 'hard-wired' to respond to the blue of twilight by settling down, becoming quiet and preparing to rest during the hours of darkness. As the body becomes less active, so mental activity is also reduced. An observant detachment becomes more apparent. As physical objects become less visible, so too the mental functions become more imaginative, vague and dreamlike. Peace descends.

the easy flow of energy

With a balance of energies within the throat chakra, peace is a tangible experience, a familiar relaxed occurrence. Where the throat chakra is stressed or blocked in some way, peace may be longed-for, but difficult, if not impossible to achieve.

Wherever there is a concentration of inappropriate energy, pressure begins to build up. Whatever the cause of the build-up, an outward flow is the only means of restoring balance, with energy flowing from an area of high pressure to one of lower

pressure. This outward flow from the body is achieved through expression and communication, via the activity of the throat chakra. If the expression is blocked in some way, the energy will have to find release through one of the other major chakra functions, for example as aggressive, selfish behaviour via the base chakra or as escapism via the brow chakra.

Singing, chanting or playing a musical instrument, even banging on a drum, will help to restore balance to the throat chakra. Toning can also be useful. This is simply making extended vowel sounds out loud for as long as your breath allows. The sound and note are less important than the quality of the vibration created through your body. Toning can be effective at releasing physical and emotional tensions. Just allow whatever sound occurs to come up, and let it go.

the need to listen

Communication is not simply about personal expression. It is also necessary to listen to what is being expressed by others. Blocks or excess energy can often distract from the true meaning of what someone else is trying to communicate, for there is a

△ **A true sense of peace arises when there is equilibrium within the chakra system and an easy flow of energy through the body.**

▽ **Drumming quietens the mind while allowing excess energy to be dissipated harmlessly through the physical activity.**

▷ Sleep and dreaming are an internal processing of many different levels of energy, requiring a balanced throat chakra to work effectively.

tendency to react to each word or phrase as it is heard, rather than comprehending the meaning of the whole.

Without the appropriate outward flow of energy there can be too much involvement with what is being communicated – everything is taken as being relevant to, or critical of, oneself. A block at the throat centre creates a closed circuit where nothing can escape. Problems also occur if individual expression has been stifled, often by overbearing discipline. When this happens the energy within the body must direct itself in one of two ways – upwards to become locked in a fantasy world of the imagination, or downwards to distort the base, sacral and solar plexus as excessive manipulation and dominance of others in overt or covert aggression.

creative expression

The resolution of such conditions is found in expressing the energy in an effective but safe manner. Any creative artistic occupation will work – as long as the focus is on the activity itself, rather than on the end product. Such activity is a release of excess energy – if a masterpiece of art is the end product this is a bonus, but it is not the intention. Not to be expressive simply because you believe that you 'can't paint' is just reinforcing the same repressive values that have probably caused the problem in the first place.

There are strategies to help you loosen artistic hang-ups that are well worth trying. One is to draw on pages from magazines or newspapers – a clean white piece of drawing paper can be intimidating. Draw with felt tip pens with broad tips. This prevents you from getting caught up with timid little lines. Alternatively, use very small pieces of paper and very fine pens - It is much easier to see your whole design and make an effective image. Set out to use all parts of the paper right up to the corners.

RELEASING PHYSICAL AND EMOTIONAL TENSION

Use this exercise to release any block that you become aware of that can be traced back to some feelings that you have not expressed. Perhaps someone has made you feel hurt or angry, and instead of confronting those feelings you have suppressed them. Burning incense of some kind while you carry out this process will help to cleanse the emotional debris from your aura and surroundings. Pungent and sweet-smelling herbs were originally used in this way for purification and to drive away demons.

1 Write down what you wish to say to the person who has hurt or angered you. As you are doing this, let any anger you are feeling find its way on to the page, allowing the feelings to come. When you have finished do not read what you have written.

2 Take the piece of paper, fold it up, and burn it in the flame of a candle or on an open fire. Simply destroy it completely. If necessary, repeat the process until you sense that your equilibrium has been restored and you can feel peace returning.

Throat chakra – getting the message

Language is the evolutionary leap that is often considered to have been the major factor in the success of our species. As a means of communicating complex concepts, planning the unknown future and sharing the experiences of the past, language has enabled us to begin living more in our minds and more in the past and the future than in the present moment. Language has given us the ability to understand what is happening to others around us. The growth of society and civilization are based on cooperation and shared dreams, which are communicated by language.

▽ The throat chakra allows us to communicate how we feel and what we think. In the West it is associated with the colour blue.

physical considerations

All the physical organs and structures of the throat have to do with letting energy move through – either inwards or outwards. The mouth, nose and throat are where we first come into contact with the air around us. Even though breathing is initiated in the solar plexus, we feel the air as it passes over the back of the palate and through the upper throat.

The mouth and oesophagus are our first contacts with food – in fact, vital digestive processes are carried out in the mouth. A great deal happens in this small area, and it all has to be carefully regulated – we are able to speak only on the outbreath as air passes over our vocal cords; we have to avoid breathing in at the same time as we swallow, or we choke.

Wrapped around the vital tubes carrying air and food – the trachea and the

△ Every form of expression reveals the emotions and thoughts of the individual, for the acknowledgement of the group.

oesophagus – are the thyroid and parathyroid glands. These major endocrine glands regulate the body's metabolism, ensuring that enough energy is produced

◁ When our inner creativity fails to emerge in the way we want, a lack of energy at the throat chakra is often the cause.

from food for our needs. Lethargy and sluggishness result from an underactive thyroid and hyperactivity is due to an overactive thyroid.

voice

The voice allows us to express what we are feeling in the heart and mind. Expressing what is going on inside ourselves to those around us gives a shared understanding and a sense of belonging. Blocks in our ability to communicate may not cause an immediate problem, as they would with the physical organs of the throat, but the curtailment of personal expression is nonetheless deeply disturbing to the energy systems as a whole. In fact, lack of expression denies our existence, our individuality ands our right to be heard.

Personal expression of ideas and thoughts, and the ability to communicate through spoken language, or the symbolic languages of writing, singing, performing or any of the other arts, help to maintain the healthy flow of energy through the throat chakra. The expression does not have to be perfect, unique or special in any way for it to be of benefit. Criticism and judgment of our expression are detrimental to the wellbeing of the chakra – indeed, if anything restricts the natural outward exuberant flow of expression, problems are likely to arise.

Indications of blocks in this area may be a stiff neck, throat infection or tension in the shoulders. Headaches or problems with swallowing or eating and metabolic disorders also point to underlying throat chakra problems. Some difficulties become obvious when frustration leads to shouting, or to its opposite: a complete withdrawal of communication.

The throat chakra is like a pressure valve. Its function is to allow the energy from the other chakra centres to express themselves so that other people can understand what is going on. If this ability is suppressed, either

USTRASANA

This exercise encourages good blood supply to the neck, keeping the energy moving through the chakra. It is a simplified version of the yoga pose ustrasana, the camel pose, which opens up the front of the body.

1 Sit on your heels on a blanket or mat, clasping your hands behind you.

2 Breathe in, then, as you breathe out, allow your head to drop backwards. At the same time, raise your arms a little behind you. Breathe normally.
3 When you are ready to release the posture, release your hands on an outbreath and bring yourself back to sitting upright.
4 Repeat this three or four times.

internally or because of outside influences, problems will inevitably arise. The chakra system works all the time as one continuous flow of energy, like cogs connected together in a machine. If one begins to seize up, all the other chakras will have their function impaired. For example, if there is a problem in a relationship, where feelings are not being acknowledged or talked about, there may be symptoms at the throat but the heart chakra will also be under strain. So if you find you are suffering from a recurrence of neck or throat problems it is always a good idea to take a look at your situation and see what restrictions might be blocking your ability to express yourself, whether they arise from others or whether you are putting unnecessary limitations on yourself.

Throat chakra – the teacher

Communication and sound are the keys to the throat chakra. Those who use these skills in their work are drawing on the energy of this centre. Through the throat we communicate how we feel inside – our emotional state – and how we think – our mental processes.

education

How effective and expressive communication is depends upon how we have been taught when still young. Many traditional forms of education pass knowledge from generation to generation through repetition and learning by rote. Very often, however, the content of the information can be misunderstood.

Many of us will be able to remember instances where hymns or prayers that were repeated regularly at home and school were misheard or just misinterpreted for many years, simply because the meaning of the words had never been explained. Communication by simple repetition has a tendency to break down very quickly, as the game known as Chinese whispers graphically illustrates.

If we, or those we talk to, are unable to understand the content of language – if we cannot 'take it to heart', true communication cannot take place. Problems with effective communication demonstrate that the chakra system has to work as an integrated whole. Without the input of the mind (the sixth and seventh chakras), and personal feelings (the heart), the throat chakra has nothing to work with.

△ Both teaching and learning use the energies of the throat chakra in the flow of communication.

teaching

The effective teacher is a person who feels excitement and interest and can express it to their students in a way that allows the knowledge to become their own. This requires an exploration of the views and opinions of others, with the possibility of dissent and disagreement. New information should be integrated with what is already known and believed, not simply asserted as inflexible dogma.

▷ Learning by doing is often more effective than learning by rote because it actively involves a broader range of chakra energies, making knowledge personal.

WHAT DO YOU BELIEVE?

This exercise is one way of looking at beliefs about yourself. Make a list of what you hold to be true beginning with 'I think that…' For example, 'I think that my feet are too big,' 'I think that I am ignored,' 'I think I talk too much,' 'I think nobody really listens to what I say,' and so on. Don't make excuses or try to rationalize or judge your statements. Very quickly, patterns will emerge that help to reveal core beliefs. Opposing views are often held simultaneously. These create internal tensions whatever viewpoint we adopt. Resolving them can free up enormous amounts of personal creativity. Discovering our inner patterns of belief reveals that we ourselves have been our teacher all along.

◁ Communication is not simply an exchange of words. Over 90 per cent of meaning is transmitted by non-verbal signals. Modern forms of communication very often excludes these important clues.

experience and what we have been told by adults. As we mature new beliefs are categorized and grouped under the relevant core beliefs. By adulthood the original core beliefs may be completely obscured by their later, more sophisticated, accretions. Still, every experience is understood in terms of the belief systems we have built up for ourselves. What we are able to hear, what we are able to understand and what we are able to express and create, all depend upon the model that we have drawn up telling us how the world works.

The throat chakra is very much the mouthpiece of the other chakras. What it listens to, what it hears and how it responds are all flavoured by the patterns of stress found within each of the other six chakras. For instance, a series of blocks within the second, sacral chakra, which brings about our sense of playful creativity, may prevent real personal creativity from being expressed via the throat chakra – even though the individual may be a wonderful narrator of other people's material.

▽ We tend to notice things that interest us, and ignore the rest. We recognize our names being spoken by others even in noisy places.

Unfortunately, when we are young, we have a tendency to believe everything that we are told. Every scrap of information is gathered and memorized in the process of getting to know how the world works. Because their language skills are still forming, children are able to sense when a conflict of information is occurring, but usually cannot express it effectively, or else they are not given the opportunity to clarify what they have been taught.

absorption

Learning to explore alternative views, even taking up opposite viewpoints in a debate, is a useful way of developing attitudes of flexibility and tolerance. Without these skills there is the danger that whatever is communicated to us will be automatically believed. Personal belief systems gradually build up in complexity as we grow. However, the basic structure is laid down when we are very young and consists of core beliefs based on personal

Throat chakra – finding your voice

The throat is traditionally associated with the element of space, which is also called ether and, in the original Sanskrit texts, akasha. This fifth element was conceived as the original container, the vessel that held all the other elements.

sound

In the original Indian texts the first thing to be created, or to emerge out of the primal space, was the vibration we call sound. These waves of sound constituted the whole of creation – all matter, all thought, all energy are in reality the interplay of the sounds or songs of the Creator. The importance of sound and speech as a creative principle is very common among the peoples of the world. Creation myths often combine the moulding of creatures out of inanimate matter with the life-giving

▽ Places of sacred significance have nearly always been chosen or constructed because of their special acoustic properties.

MANTRA CHANTING

△ Although mantras often have meaning their real value is in the quality of subtle sound they create within the body.

Chanting and using mantra meditation offer ways of releasing throat chakra problems and experiencing finer levels of speech. Mantras are powerful sequences of sound that enliven deep levels of energy in the body and mind. Traditionally, mantras are chosen by a teacher to be appropriate to the individual. It is important not to use 'any old sound' as a mantra, as this can have a disruptive effect on subtle levels. The primal sound in many traditions is 'AAAH' – the first vowel sound that is made with a completely relaxed throat. Taking a deep breath and simply chanting AAAH for as long as possible creates a clearing in the throat chakra. Begin loud and after a few repetitions, start to chant more softly, until the sound is simply a thought, then a silence in the mind.

▷ **The soothing sound of storytelling trains the mind to understand many nuances of meaning and language.**

addition of breath or the process of naming. Myths and stories show the magical and spiritual significance of knowing the right names for things.

truth

Where it is functioning at its highest level the throat chakra should be bringing out our own truth into the world. Truth is not just a matter of correct information. Neither does truth carry any moral weight, though it can be experienced as good or bad, comfortable or uncomfortable, depending on how it interacts with each person's beliefs about what is real. Each of us will dismiss as untrue those things that do not fall within our personal construction of how the universe works.

Speaking from a level of personal truth means that whatever is said carries the conviction of our whole being, sometimes referred to as will. Personal will or truth rarely emerges however, because we are all constrained by the values and concepts we have been taught by others. All our communications are filtered and distorted by the many energy blocks that have arisen from the stresses and traumas of the past. Only with the gradual removal of these stresses can a more honest and open relationship with the world emerge.

lies, damned lies…

Telling lies has a remarkable effect on the whole body. When a lie is told, conflict in the hemispheres of the brain releases stress hormones that create measurable changes in blood chemistry and skin resistance, and a dip in all the subtle energies of the meridians and subtle bodies. The throat chakra energies become strained and distorted if lying becomes habitual. Lying is

never successful, simply because the stress it causes cannot be totally disguised, but is communicated to the observer at subconscious levels, thereby arousing doubt and suspicion.

Fear, doubt and uncertainty all prevent honest, open communication. We can try to avoid telling lies, but until fear is removed completely all behaviour will be a compromise between what an individual really wants and what they perceive is required by others. By working to clear the throat chakra, these oppressive blocks to creativity and true expression of self can gradually be dissipated.

The best known mantra is probably OM. It consists of three sounds A-U-M, each of which expresses in seed form the creation of everything in the universe. AAAH is the most natural sound to emerge from the mouth. The O sound begins to shape and control this open flow of energy, symbolizing the creation of form. The M, actually a nasal hum closer to -NG, represents the continuity of the complex vibrations that make up the many levels of reality. The Tibetan mantra OM-AA-HUNG is a variation of this primal sound and can be used as a regular exercise to cleanse the

▽ **The formal characters of the Tibetan alphabet spell out the primal sounds OM, AA, HUNG, encapsulating every aspect of creation.**

chakras, open the throat and quieten the mind. It can be done without accompanying visualization, though introducing the other elements adds significantly to the effect.

1 Take a good breath and sound an OM for as long as you can without straining, rhyming it with 'from'. At the same time visualize white light at the centre of the brow, or the Tibetan character for this sound.
2 Now take another deep breath and pronounce AA, rhyming it with 'car'. Continue for as long as you can. At the same time see red light at the centre of the throat or the character for this sound, coloured red.
3 On the third breath, sound HUNG, rhyming it with 'sung'. End the sound by humming with your mouth closed so that your skull bones vibrate. With this sound visualize a blue light at the heart or a blue Tibetan symbol for the sound. Repeat the sequence as many times as you like.

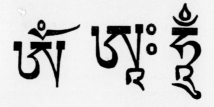

Brow chakra – seeing the picture

The chakra located in the centre of the forehead is called ajña, meaning to perceive and to command. It is directly related to the senses of sight and hearing, although all three upper chakras – the throat, brow and crown – are physically close together and share many correspondences. Throat chakra influences extend to the mouth and jaw and up to the ears, while the brow has more links with the face, eyes, nose and forehead. The neck and base of the skull can be influenced by both brow and throat energies. Crown chakra energies relate to the cranium, the bones of the top of the head at and above the hairline.

▽ **The brow chakra is the seat of understanding, from where we picture how the world is.**

thoughts

Our everyday awareness is located in the area of the brow chakra, from where our higher sense functions scan the world around us. The consciousness of self, of the unique personality of the mind, is felt to be seated here, like a commander at his control post. We are very much in our heads – more than, say, in our heart or our solar plexus. The physical body belongs to us but we do not think of it as being 'us' in the same way.

We relate to our own thoughts, our interpretations and inner conversations, continually assessing the information that feeds in through the senses. We relate to others by focusing attention on the face – the eyes and the subtle changes of expression, feeling that the 'real person' is somewhere in there. This arises from the awareness that here at the brow chakra we

△ **Perception is understanding how different parts come together to make a whole. It is the job of the brow chakra to interpret clearly.**

begin to make sense of and interpret the world. The brow chakra is all about seeing, not just seeing with the eyes, but seeing with the mind – making sense of and understanding what is being perceived.

eyesight

We do not see what the eyes see. The eye focuses light through the lens and an upside-down image is thrown on to the retina at the back of the eye. However, only one tiny spot, the fovea, has a concentration of light-sensitive cells great enough to produce a complete focused image; the rest of the eye receives a vaguer, more blurred picture. Rapid movement of the eyes adds more

CLEAR SEEING

Seeing clearly depends on the coordination between the mind and the eyes. Confusion in understanding (seeing) arises when blocks in the brow chakra disturb the complex relationship between eye movements and nerve impulses as they travel to the centres of visual comprehension in the brain. Getting confused shows that stress is affecting coordination. Practice will re-open these pathways, increasing your ability to focus and understand the world around you. This simple exercise helps both the muscles controlling eye movement and the balance between the left and right hemispheres of the brain.

▽ **Seeing is not simply a sense of perception. We use 'I see' to mean 'I understand'. Seeing relies on the flexibility of the mind as well as the sharpness of the eyes.**

1 Sit in a relaxed position with an upright head. Gaze forwards with your eyes relaxed.
2 Turn your eyes upwards and as high as they will go, making sure your head does not move. Now slowly and attentively roll your eyes in a clockwise direction.
3 When you return to the top again, relax and gaze forward for a moment.
4 Now repeat the exercise, but this time move your eyes anticlockwise, in the opposite direction to before. Make sure your head remains still and that your eyes move as slowly and evenly as possible.
5 Repeat each cycle a couple of times unless you feel some strain. If you want to check your eye-brain coordination, do this exercise while you are saying a nursery rhyme or counting numbers.

of memories, the brain organizes the visual information so that we can understand and really 'see'. Perception is the art of creating order from potential chaos, from random impulses. Perception is the main function of the brow chakra.

Balancing this chakra can help physical problems with the eyes, but more than this, it will help remove confusion caused by an inability to distinguish important things from insignificant ones; in visual terms, the foreground from the background. Clear seeing, understanding and perspective are all mental skills that are needed to interpret visual data, as well as the mental pictures that are our thoughts, memories and ideas.

Seeing the picture allows us to move within the orderly, familiar patterns of life. Without the brow chakra making sense of information received by the brain, we would be paralysed by confusion and indecision.

▽ **Pattern-making is essential for the mind to understand what it is being shown by the eyes. Whenever possible a pattern will be seen, even in a random display of colours.**

information, scanning the field of vision to allow us to get a clearer set of images. When these images travel to the brain they are switched, so that information from the left eye travels to the right hemisphere of the brain and vice versa.

breaking the code

The brain interprets the flurry of electrical nerve impulses and fills in all the gaps itself. Recognizing familiar shapes and relationships between things, creating patterns that mean something from its store

Brow chakra – creative dreaming

The colour associated with the brow chakra is indigo – the deep blue of a midnight sky. It is the colour of deep silence and stillness, of resonant emptiness and solitude. The brow chakra has a certain degree of detachment from emotional concerns.

perspective

In order to see clearly, a distance must be maintained between subject and object. It is possible to recognize patterns only when the background, known as the field, is empty. In the same way, the emotions at the brow chakra have to be quiet in order to allow clear images to appear. Because the process of seeing involves so much 'filling in' by the brain, any strong emotional involvement can distort the picture we receive and our eyes can deceive us. If our emotional needs are too strong it is possible to become obsessed with the fine details of the pattern so that nothing else is seen – the 'big picture' is lost in the power of a single idea or dream. Silence and detachment allow the brow chakra to keep its perspective.

▽ **Time and space are laws of physical reality that do not constrain the non-physical worlds of the mind and spirit. All things become possible.**

detachment

Jumping to conclusions and making assumptions are signs that the brow chakra is becoming confused by too much emotional noise, blurring the clear distinction between 'I want' and 'I see'. Allowing the spaciousness of detached and passive watching increases the possibility that intuition – the flash of knowing that seems to come from nowhere – will arise in the mind. Receptivity and openness to new possibilities allow the necessary clarity in the brow for accurate perception.

Detachment is crucial to the functioning of the brow chakra at all levels, not just at the emotional level. Mental agility requires the ability to step back from the normal waking experiences of time and space. Where the throat chakra uses sound to communicate in language – a linear, time-based experience – the brow chakra uses light to carry messages in the form of visual symbols and pictures. The internal world of dreams, daydreams and the imagination is not limited by the rules of the physical universe. Anything can appear: the impossible alongside the mundane, the fantastic with the ordinary. As in dreams, the logic of time and matter can be ignored.

△ **Making sense of things requires the perspective of distance to see the whole picture. Taking a rest from problems allows the ajña to see new patterns that may give solutions.**

Transformations occur continually, changing scenes and context. Events can happen simultaneously or even run backwards in time. From the perspective of conscious awareness all this is confusing and difficult to understand. From the perspective of the mental functioning of the brow chakra this language of light is a straightforward communication of energy that directly affects the electrical impulses of the brain, and from there, the whole system.

The brow chakra, resting in its state of quiet observation, can build up, interpret and change the very nature of our reality. It is no wonder that its Sanskrit name, ajña, also means 'one who commands'. The new discipline of psychoneuro-immunology is a medical adaptation of the visualization techniques of yogis and mystics who, through experience, knew full well the power of the mind to alter every aspect of the body and the physical world by constructing meaningful images of light within their own minds.

MATSYASANA

Here are two versions of an exercise that can help to focus energy at the brow chakra. Try both versions and choose whichever is the most comfortable or effective for you.

The name for this posture, the fish, comes from Matsya, the name for the fish incarnation of Vishnu, the Hindu deity who is the source and maintainer of the universe and everything in it.

1 For the first version (left), begin by kneeling on a blanket or mat. Place the palms of your hands on the floor behind you, fingers pointing forwards, bending your elbows.

2 Lean back on to your elbows and breathe in. As you breathe out, let your head drop backwards and arch your back slightly. Breathe normally, focusing on your brow chakra.

3 For the second version (below), sit with your legs out in front of you and your feet together. Place the palms of your hands under your hips, bending your elbows behind you.

4 Lean back on to your elbows and breathe in. As you breathe out, lean backwards until you are supporting yourself on your arms. Allow your head to drop backwards and arch your back slightly. Breathe normally, again focusing on your brow chakra.

5 When you are ready to come out of this position, allow your elbows to slide away, lowering yourself to a lying position.

6 Roll on to your side and sit up.

Brow chakra – visions

In popular thought the brow chakra is considered to be synonymous with the 'third eye'. In traditional Indian texts the forehead has many interrelated smaller chakras, which extend upwards from the ajña between the eyebrows until they merge with the functions of the crown chakra. Each of these chakras deals with increasingly fine experiences of perception, clarity and realms of subtle energy where deities and other powerful spirits dwell. The sixth and seventh chakras enable consciousness to move beyond the physical universe. To the ardent materialist of the 21st century, reality is objective solidity. What happens in the mind, not being physical or measurable in any way, is illusory, ephemeral, subjective. In fact, normal reality is largely a mind-created construct that can only be experienced subjectively, within ourselves.

insight and intuition

Intuition is hard to define, but can be understood as a prompting from all the levels of awareness beyond the everyday conscious mind, which some would associate with the unconscious or subconscious mind. Intuition presents a whole picture, an overview and an understanding that goes beyond the simple explanation of its parts. The whole picture given us in a flash of intuition brings a sense of solidity, of usefulness to the mind. Giving ourselves space to notice and act on intuitive insight frees the energy of the brow chakra. Confidence in the subtle signals received from these areas of perception can develop into 'clear seeing' or clairvoyance.

clairvoyance

The clairvoyant experience is not necessarily only a visual one; it is 'clear seeing' in the sense of receiving clear, penetrating insight. The knowledge that accompanies the act of clairvoyance may include visual data, but these are not necessarily perceived in the same way that we see the everyday world. The information is more akin to dream imagery and memory. The attention travels, or moves beyond time and space, to visualize new information. For many people, it seems difficult to distinguish clairvoyance from imagination, and is usually referred to as 'only my imagination', as if it should be instantly discounted as an unsafe source of information. With experience and an increase in confidence the difference can be felt quite clearly – it is as though different mental muscles have come into play.

How we receive information depends very much on the way we naturally interpret our senses. Psychologists recognize three distinct types of response that we all possess, though we favour one over the others. A visual imagination will find it very easy to see thoughts in terms of pictures, in clear detail and full colour. A kinaesthetic imagination will interpret thoughts and images as feelings, either as moods or as sensations related to the body. An auditory imagination will interpret information as words, phrases or dialogue.

Recognizing which type we are makes it easier to identify the prompting of the brow chakra's intuition for what it is. For example, with a kinaesthetic mind it is no good expecting to see clear images. With a visual mind it is important to learn how the mind employs symbols, whereas with an auditory mind, thoughts pop into the head.

▽ The brow chakra has the ability to see beyond the obvious, accessing the realms of intuition and clairvoyance to gain insight.

PSYCHOMETRY

This exercise provides a way of receiving impressions about an object, its history and owners. It is best carried out with an open curiosity and a sense of fun. Don't worry about getting it right or wrong, just play with the possibilities. Practise with objects from many different people and places, and you will quickly develop your accuracy and the strength of your impressions.

1 Ask a friend for a piece of jewellery or a watch. If it is old and has had more than one owner, all the better. Sit comfortably and allow your breathing to settle, then turn your attention inwards and allow your senses to still.

2 Pick up the object, hold it in your hands and focus on it. Begin to process your thoughts, feelings and any sensations or imagery that come to you.

3 To deepen the process you might find it helpful to place the item against your brow chakra. After a minute or so put the object down. Turn your attention to yourself once again, allowing your breathing to settle. Turn your attention to the soles of your feet for a minute to ground your energy, then relate your impressions.

Crown chakra – the fountain head

The Sanskrit name for the crown chakra is sahasrara, meaning 'thousandfold'. This refers to the image of the thousand-petalled lotus which, in Hindu thought, represents the epitome of the human condition. The chakra is described as being positioned just above the head.

the pituitary gland

The gland most often associated with the crown chakra is the pituitary, though some texts do quote the relevant gland as being

▽ The crown chakra is the main coordinating centre of the body and ensures that the individual is also connected to universal sources of energy.

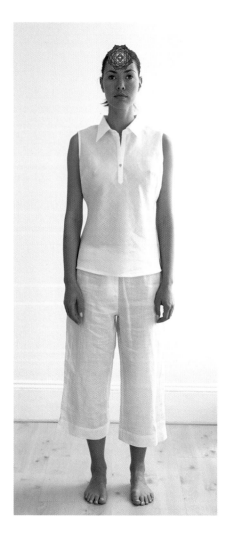

the pineal. The pituitary gland is located at the base of the brain. It has two sections, the anterior and posterior, which are each responsible for releasing particular hormones. The pituitary is often referred to as the 'master gland' because it affects so many other glands and body functions.

the brain

The brain is a most complex organ with four main sections and billions of nerves. One section of the brain, the cerebrum, is involved with sensation, reasoning, planning and problem solving. The diencephalon contains the pineal gland, the thalamus and the hypothalamus, which are referred to collectively as the limbic system. This controls body temperature, water balance, appetite, heart rate, sleep patterns and emotions. The brain stem, midbrain, pons and medulla oblongata control breathing, heart rate and blood pressure. The cerebellum controls posture, balance and the coordination of the muscles that are associated with movement.

coordination

From the viewpoint of physical health, the crown chakra is mostly concerned with coordination. Coordination is needed at all levels. Individual cells within the pituitary gland and the diencephalon have to coordinate to ensure the smooth running of the bodily functions. The cerebellum is responsible for helping us to coordinate our muscles to achieve balance, posture and movement.

Coordination skills are learned at an early age – and reinforced by crawling on all-fours. Research in the last 30 years has shown that children who do not crawl on all-fours in infancy often experience coordination difficulties as they grow up. It has been found that returning to this early form of locomotion, even as an adult, can assist the cerebellum in gaining full muscle control. It has also been discovered that

CROSS CRAWL

This exercise can be fun if your approach is playful, and especially if you have problems coordinating your arms and legs, or even your thought patterns.

1 Stand up straight, but relaxed.
2 Lift up and bend your right knee.
3 As you do this, bring your left hand to your chin.
4 Bring your left elbow and right knee into contact or as close as you can.
5 Lower your right leg, relax your left arm.
6 Lift up and bend your left knee.

7 As you do this, bring your right hand to your chin, bending the right elbow.
8 Bring the right elbow and left knee into contact or as close as you can.
9 This is one cycle. Repeat fairly quickly 10–30 times.

ADHO MUKHA SVANASANA

The dog posture helps to balance the energy between the feet and the crown chakra.

1 Kneel on a non-slip surface on all-fours, making sure your knees are in a straight line under your hips. Make sure your hands are in a straight line under your shoulders and spread your fingers. Tuck your toes under.
2 Breathe in, lifting your pelvis and straightening your legs, keeping your head low.

3 Breathe naturally. As you stay in the posture, imagine your bottom is lifting upwards, but your heels are lowering to the floor, stretching your back.
4 When you decide to release the posture, breathe in, then as you breathe out, lower yourself back on to all-fours.
5 Slide yourself back until you are sitting on your heels, rest your forehead on the floor and relax for a few moments.

△ The well-known test of rubbing your stomach while tapping your head is a good example of body-mind coordination.

▽ Activities such as balancing and juggling require whole-brain coordination. Balance in life demands whole-chakra coordination.

many types of learning difficulties can be helped by exercises that utilize opposite parts of the body, confirming that brain coordination and function can be improved.

Coordination problems can occur on many levels throughout life. Physical difficulties like poor balance or clumsiness are quite obvious manifestations of the problem. Dyslexia often results from poor coordination between brain hemispheres, as the eyes move across a page of writing or scan down a text. On a less obvious level, coordination with the world as a whole is also a function of the crown chakra. Finding yourself at the right place at the right time, or just happening to meet the one person you were needing to speak to, having lucky coincidences and strange sequences of events that all work out very well, are signs that your crown chakra is feeding you good information.

Crown chakra – the illusion of detachment

The development of expanded awareness underpins the crown chakra at the emotional level. The opportunity to understand our individual role in the world does not present itself until our teenage years, when we start to move away from the family base.

Growing up in a balanced way, developing adults use the lessons from childhood to create a sense of unity and empathy with people around them. Service to others is often thought to be truly selfless, but there may be hidden motives. We often serve others so we can feel useful and needed, or to create an ideal world where we don't have to see people suffer. We may also see others as more worthy of being cared for than ourselves, diverting attention away from our own needs. Helping those less fortunate can sometimes suppress a sense of our individuality. The loss of personal identity can lead to feeling overwhelmed.

negative attachment

Many philosophies encourage us to free ourselves from emotional 'attachment' in order to achieve spiritual goals. However, the state of being 'non-attached' sometimes acts as a mask for a refusal to accept personal

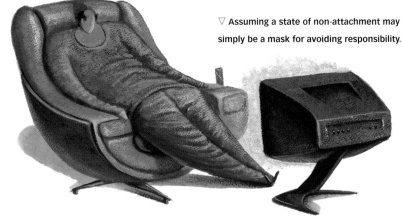

▽ **Assuming a state of non-attachment may simply be a mask for avoiding responsibility.**

▽ **When there is a lack of awareness of personal needs, it is easy for the enthusiastic helper to be a martyr to idealism.**

responsibility. The need to renounce or escape from the responsibility of the family, work or the world in general must be carefully examined for its real motive. Though a change in direction may seem to offer more personal freedom, it could be that working within the current situation could provide a better opportunity for growth. Being emotionally attached to something is sometimes bound up with a fearful unwillingness to allow that thing to change. This closes down other possibilities.

The crown chakra is concerned with openness, and when you get over-attached to a closed way of thinking or feeling, this will tend to prevent you from dealing with reality. The remedy is to be compassionate with yourself and consider all possibilities. Unless this open compassion is first directed towards yourself, allowing healing at the crown chakra, it is impossible to be truly compassionate.

reality and fantasy

With the upper chakras, particularly the brow and crown chakras, there are a lot of fine or subtle energies coming into play. Because we often feel restricted by the inflexibility of the three-dimensional world (things take time and effort to accomplish, plans go wrong, and so on), there can be a certain attractiveness in the ephemeral quality of these areas of consciousness. The lack of restrictions, the breadth of possibilities, the sense of freedom can work a powerful magic on those dissatisfied with the world of here and now.

For those not drawn to metaphysics and philosophy this might manifest as retreat into a fantasy world of imagination. In a dominant personality where the base chakra is still strong, this imbalance might become a dogmatic idealism or even a megalomania.

An interest in spirituality has the potential to open new awareness of thought and activity that can really help people to break out of old behaviour patterns and become more fulfilled. But equally it can trap us in a web of glamour filled with bright, shiny, amazing things that can never be grasped for long enough to integrate usefully into life. Balance is always achieved where all the chakras are able to perform efficiently. For example, when we are truly grounded, rooted in the secure energies of the base chakra, it will be possible to experience finer, less tangible qualities of reality without losing perspective.

OPENING UP

Sometimes it can be difficult to imagine how we could continue in life without someone or something. We may have become over-dependent on a person, a way of living or a belief. This exercise will help you to open your life to new possibilities.

1 Identify a person, situation or belief that you are overly or fearfully attached to.

2 Sit for a minute or two, allowing your thoughts and emotions to dwell on the issue.

3 Note down on a sheet of paper all the things you can think of that embody that attachment.

4 If it is a person: note their qualities, what they give you, what you feel you may lose if they go.

5 If it is a situation: note what it is you value about it, what status it gives you, why you need it.

6 If it is a belief, thought or feeling: note what will change if it is no longer with you, and try to include why it is that you fear this.

7 Look at what you have written. Try to discover the games you have been playing with yourself, or the stories you have been allowing yourself to believe. Sit with this for a few minutes, with your eyes away from your notes, then look again at what you have written.

8 Close your eyes and imagine all the illusions, untruths or problems you have discovered filling a large bubble in front of you.

9 When the bubble is full, imagine it floating slowly up into a cloudless sky and dispersing.

Crown chakra – thought

Thought processes associated with the crown chakra fall into two main categories: how we think the world operates and those thoughts linking us to the universal scheme of things. Our beliefs about the world, our role in it and what we expect from the world form the basis of a behavioural programme that affects all our chakras. We build up a store of beliefs from our experiences in the world. However, thoughts linking us to the wider universe tend to be less easy to identify, and often surface through dreams and meditation. What we expect, especially what we fear, has a knack of being drawn towards us in some way.

reactions

The way we interpret events and then react to them is the reason why our lives progress or falter in the way they do. For example, suppose you trap your fingers in a door. The possible reactions are:

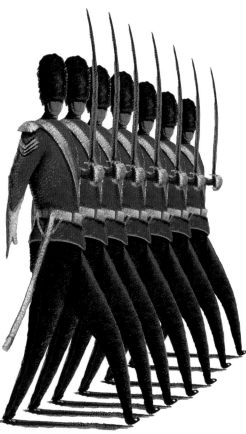

TUNING IN

The crown chakra enables us to move into realms beyond the physical universe, and this exercise is useful for beginning to co-create a dialogue with an image of a deity or archetype. Sit in a chair, with an empty chair nearby. Imagine an image of a deity or archetype that you strongly relate to, seated in the empty chair. Think of a question or a situation you are encountering where you would appreciate guidance. Pose the question to the image. Close your eyes and sit quietly for a minute or two, then see yourself in the other chair as the image you created. Bearing in mind the question, answer it as spontaneously as you can. If you do not get an answer, don't worry. It is likely that thoughts in the next few hours or dreams overnight will shed some light on your question.

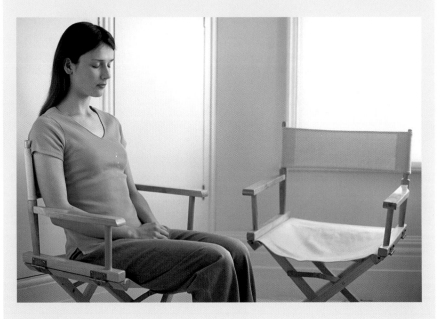

1 No reaction.
2 An exclamation followed by personal thoughts that you should have been more careful.
3 An exclamation followed by berating yourself for always being so stupid.
4 Slamming the door, blaming the person in front of you or behind you.
5 Hitting the person behind you because it was their fault.

◁ **A society that makes no space for personal revelation runs the risk of becoming repressive and stagnant.**

Each reaction to a stimulus reveals your programming concerning that stimulus, and at the same time reinforces that programming. Your reaction also determines how the world reacts back. In the case of the trapped fingers, options 4 and 5 would be likely to invite a negative riposte, escalating the situation further.

universal links

The crown chakra is our link to the universal sources of energy and information. In a natural maturing process the adolescent or young adult will begin to look for

△ The desire to expand and grow is inherent in all chakras, from the base right up to the crown, where its connection to universal energy reminds us constantly that more is possible.

answers to questions such as 'Why am I here?' that initiate the search for greater knowledge. Unfortunately this natural progression can be seriously hampered by family, social and religious backgrounds that do not accept individual exploration. In extreme cases, most traditions contain groups or factions whose fundamentalist, sexist or authoritarian practices instil shame, fear and self-disgust into children who question the status quo. This repression effectively disconnects people from their personal links with spirituality of any type. Children who are experiencing these sorts of restrictions need to break through them or they will find it impossible to develop as individuals and reach their full potential. When the crown chakra is prevented from working normally it is unable to provide all the energy and information required by the other chakras.

A healthy crown chakra is finely balanced on all levels. The thoughts that come and go need to be allowed free passage. It is only when we try to hold on to thoughts, without allowing alternatives or the possibility of change, that disruption of the crown chakra happens.

◁ Trying to control the thoughts of others is like trying to stop clouds moving across the sky. Holding on to another's way of thinking is as misguided.

LITTLE YOGA NIDRA

This exercise, yoga sleep, combines the ability to visualize with the flow of information and energy throughout the body. Sit or lie in a comfortable position and relax for a few minutes, allowing your breathing to slow.

1 Take your attention down to your left big toe. Don't move it, but be aware of it as a focus for the mind.
2 Shift the focus in turn to your second, third, fourth and fifth toes. Then to the ball of the foot, instep, top of the foot and left heel.
3 Carry on to the lower leg, the back of the knee, the top of the knee, top of the thigh, back of the thigh and left buttock.
4 Take your attention down to your right big toe, second, third, fourth and fifth toes; the ball of the foot, instep, top of the foot and heel; lower leg, back of the knee, top of the knee, top of the thigh, back of the thigh and right buttock.
5 Take the attention to the left side of your back, the left side from hip to armpit and the left side of the chest. Then to the right side of your back, right side from hip to armpit, right side of the chest.
6 Take your attention to your left thumb. Then first finger, second, third and fourth; the palm of your hand, back of the hand, wrist, inside of the elbow, outside of the elbow, upper arm, left shoulder.
7 Then to your right thumb; first, second, third and fourth finger; the palm of your hand, back of the hand, wrist, inside of the elbow, outside of the elbow, upper arm and right shoulder.
8 On to your head and neck; left side of your face, right side of your face; left ear, right ear; left eye, right eye; mouth, inside the mouth.
9 At the end you should be feeling totally relaxed. You can repeat it if you are particularly tense or find it hard to relax.

Crown chakra – unity

△ With the crown chakra cleared of stresses, a sense of lightness, clarity and belonging flows through the whole chakra system.

▽ The series of poses, or asanas, that are undertaken during the practice of hatha yoga are designed to prepare the body for meditation.

The crown chakra focuses on what we experience as well as what we know or understand. If each level of each chakra has been integrated, the crown chakra represents illumination. Unless we truly understand what we see we are unable to apply our creative skills, fulfilling our visions of what is possible. The more we fulfil our visions, the more our consciousness expands, the more we understand what we see, and so on, in ever-increasing awareness.

yoga

Meditation is a key to the process of increasing awareness. In traditional Hindu philosophies, meditation is undertaken only when the body and mind have been harnessed towards that goal. This is the purpose of yoga, in particular raja yoga, also known as the eight-fold path. The steps or 'limbs' are sequential challenges or tasks:

1 Yama – 'general behaviour'. The student is expected to follow the disciplines that are said to be the foundation of an ethical society: ahimsa (non-violence), satya (speaking the truth), asteya (not envying or stealing), brahmacharya (not wasting

TRATAK
This is usually practised using a lighted candle as a focus, but you can use anything, like a flower or a stone. Although at first it may cause your eyes to run, it is used to improve eyesight. Place the object at eye level about an arm's length away from you.

Close your eyes and settle your breathing. Open your eyes and look steadily at the item. Try not to strain. After a minute, close your eyes. Visualize the item in your heart chakra or at the brow chakra. When the image fades, open your eyes and repeat.

▷ Many people who think that they cannot meditate, have simply not found a technique that suits them. Traditional techniques include gazing at an object (tratak), use of sound (mantra) and use of shape or geometry (yantra).

resources), aparigraha (not hoarding what you don't need).

2 Niyama – 'observances'. The student should achieve the following: saucha (purity), santosha (contentment), tapas (effort), svadhyaya (spiritual study), isvara pranidhana (dedication of all activity to higher divine forces).

3 Asana – 'postures'. Physical exercises prepare the body for sitting in meditation.

4 Pranayama – 'breath control'. Breathing techniques control and redirect the life-force around the body.

5 Pratyahara – 'sense control'. This focuses on reaching an understanding of how the mind works so that unwanted tendencies can be weeded out.

6 Dharana – 'concentration'. This is the preparation of the mind for meditation.

7 Dhyana – 'meditation': the ultimate goal.

8 Samadhi – 'union': the fruit of all the preceding practices.

meditation

Although raja yoga may seem rigid and austere to Westerners, there is logic in it. When all the steps are followed, meditation comes more easily. If you simply decide you are going to meditate and sit down and expect your body, emotions and mind to comply, you will be very lucky if they do so for more than a few minutes, if that.

The mind is a wonderfully restless, inventive faculty and cannot be reined in without great understanding or cunning. Good meditation techniques offer the mind something to do to keep it occupied or active in a tight focus that enables us to experience ourselves in the gaps between thoughts. The more we experience the gap between the thoughts, the more relaxed our bodies become and the more clearly we can see how our thoughts shape our lives.

▷ The crown chakra is the source of all chakra energies in the same way that white light is the source of the rainbow spectrum.

Keeping the
Balance

To be effective and long-lasting, chakra healing needs to keep in view a unified picture of the system. The chakras are dynamic energies that represent the whole person, so chakra healing must also deal with the whole person.

The dynamics of harmony

The chakra system is complex and interrelated – each chakra, both major and minor, can be thought of as a cog in a machine. A change in the movement of one will create changes throughout the whole structure. There will be an efficient flow of energy when all parts are locked together in their activity, working harmoniously together. If one chakra becomes damaged or has its normal range of activity restricted this inevitably puts strain on its closest neighbours, which will also begin to suffer.

A chakra that becomes unbalanced has become stuck at an inappropriate level of activity. It is either working with insufficient energy for its task, or it is working too hard. In either circumstance the other chakras will have to compensate by changing their levels of energy. This means that the system as a whole will be working at one level when it may be more appropriate for it to function at another.

overall balance

The chakra system, like the rest of the body, responds to the circumstances of its environment. In some circumstances a particular chakra will tend to take a larger role, but it should still operate in a balanced way within the normal working parameters of the system.

Different jobs and lifestyles need special areas of expertise, and the dynamics of the chakras need to adjust accordingly. For example, a singer will naturally need to have an especially active throat chakra to keep the voice healthy. The heart chakra, too, will need to have plenty of energy to foster a depth of feeling,

△ All parts of the chakra system respond to changes in every other part. Releasing stress from one area will help to relax the whole system, making everything run better.

empathy and personal involvement in the work. In such a person, an observer who was sensitive to energy fields would see a lot of activity at those two centres. Only if too much energy is focused in one area will problems start to show, beginning in

▷ False equilibrium is where a temporary stability has been achieved. However, even a slight change will bring about a breakdown in order. When this occurs in the chakra system, illness may develop.

◁ **Crystals, with their brilliant colour and unique structures are very effective ways to bring balance to the chakra system.**

those places where there are natural weaknesses as a result of past stresses or current overuse.

The chakra system will change gear with a change of activity. Meditation requires a different sort of energy from cooking the dinner; playing a musical instrument requires different skills from listening to an orchestra; escaping from a stressful situation uses different resources from gazing at a serene sunset. Problems arise when, through stress of one sort or another, the chakra system fails to change gear and becomes stuck in a single mode of functioning.

Throughout our lives, stresses of many sorts accumulate in all our systems, from physical to spiritual. These stresses can be like grains of sand or grit that create a little roughness in the workings of our chakra cogs, or they can be like a spanner that seriously throws the whole mechanism out of alignment.

considerations

In learning about the symptoms of chakra imbalance presented here and in other books, it is important not to become disheartened about your own state of energetic health. At one time or another most of us will experience extremes of under- and overactivity in all our chakras. It is more important to recognize the common tendencies that are repeated through our lives. Once the most prevalent states are known they can be worked on and necessary alterations can begin to be made.

A physical balancing technique can have a beneficial effect on an emotional chakra stress, and a mental visualization exercise can allow positive change to happen at a physical, everyday level. So use those techniques and exercises that you find most helpful and that fit most comfortably into your everyday life.

Many traditional systems of spiritual development take into account the differences between individuals and their lifestyles, providing different sorts of practices to suit their needs. Today we are lucky in having a wide range of chakra balancing techniques from all around the world. Even the most hectic lifestyle can accommodate sufficient practices to help to reduce the burden of stress that overloads the chakra system and will eventually lead to health problems. The only thing that is needed is for us to set aside a little time dedicated to our own repair. This is largely a process of developing a habit. At first, all sorts of

distractions may arise until the routine becomes a natural part of our day. Most balancing practices need a little effort and dedication in the beginning – not only to bring in a new routine, but also because we are beginning to make changes in our energy systems.

Correcting a false equilibrium requires skill and patience. Like a tightrope walker who has been working for years with a pole that has a large weight at one end and nothing on the other end, we adjust to the weight of stress we have accumulated in our lives in order to continue as best we can. Removing all the stress in one go may seem to be the best solution but, like the tightrope walker, we need to familiarize ourselves gradually with the new state of balance at each step. If not, the risk increases that we will feel less secure than we did when we had all the stress.

Like kicking an addictive habit, the biggest problem most of us face is that habitual patterns of behaviour feel comfortable and part of our true personality. Working with a balancing system that focuses on the different levels of body, mind and emotion can be helpful in maintaining an even development of chakra healing. Traditional methods like yoga, Tai Chi and Chi Kung all have outer, physical activities that release stress from the body. They also have mental techniques that involve meditative states, or visualizations that help to clarify the subtle energies of the mind and emotions. It is important to pay attention to all these different levels of practice. For example, it will be of limited value to have a body that is supple and toned if you are still emotionally insecure or stuck in some past trauma.

Contemporary techniques, such as crystal therapy, colour therapy and flower essences, can help to remove specific stresses in chakra centres as well as bringing the whole body into a better state of balance.

Maintaining harmony

The more our energy systems are brought into harmonious balance, the easier it is to maintain that balance. An old, worn engine is so full of leaks and random rattles it is hard to notice any new disturbing sounds of dysfunction. With a engine that runs smoothly the slightest drop in efficiency is noticed immediately and can be put right.

exploration

Until some of the stresses can be removed from the chakra system, every one of us will be so busy maintaining our false sense of equilibrium that there will be little spare energy for exploring individual potential. Learning to expand into life is what the evolution of the chakras from base to crown shows us. Getting stuck in any one area narrows our perspective on life. Rather than being able to explore the world with seven different lenses, each with its own special abilities to filter and magnify our experience, we can find ourselves with a single obsessive keyhole through which we squint in an eager attempt to find out what

▽ When all chakras are free of stress the individual also becomes free to move in whatever direction is of most benefit.

△ A balanced and sensitive chakra system will recognize any upset and be able to restore proper functioning automatically.

▷ Taking time to balance your chakras is giving time back to your life, so that you will be better able to achieve your goals.

our life has really been missing. In reality we have all the keys to all the doorways within us at all times. The chakra system is much more than a line of coloured spheres reflecting our bodies' other functions.

opening doorways

As the ancient yogis of India and Tibet discovered, clearing the chakras of the build-up of debris allows life to be entirely transformed – not by escapist fantasy but by the clear, honest experience of reality as satisfying and nourishing. In this state each chakra becomes a translucent doorway allowing a free flow of universal energies in and out of the body. False boundaries and a frustrating sense of separation dissolve because it was only the stress and imbalance that created them in the first place.

The chakra system always works in two apparently opposite directions. From the base chakra upwards there is an increasing experience of expansion, from the focus and solidity of physical matter, through experience of sensation, personal power, relationship with the rest of the world, communication, understanding and finally integration on all levels at the crown chakra.

Simultaneously there is a flow of energy towards the grounding solidity of physical reality, from the timeless and directionless unity of the crown chakra through

the defining vision of the brow, the form-giving quality of naming, a stabilizing relationship between the self and the world, learning how to control one's power, exploring the senses and finally being able to mould and create the raw material of the world – the practical energy of the base chakra.

In the same way that the individual chakras reflect and balance one another,

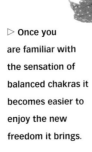

▷ Once you are familiar with the sensation of balanced chakras it becomes easier to enjoy the new freedom it brings.

each relying on the others in equal measure, the two opposing tides are part of one process, where expansion into the spiritual realms can be effective only with a reciprocal exploration into the universe of matter.

Whether you consider yourself to be a spiritual or a pragmatic person, whether your goals in life are based on material success or spiritual fulfilment, whether you are a steel-worker or an aromatherapist, a teenager or an octagenarian, learning to heal and work with the chakras is one of the most effective routes to wellbeing.

Salute to the sun

The salute to the sun is a traditional sequence of exercises from hatha yoga that systematically activates the energies of each chakra. Practised regularly, it can help to energize each chakra and then keep them all in balance. Traditionally this sequence is practised as the sun rises.

1 Begin by deep breathing for two to five minutes.

▽ 2 Stand upright and bring your palms together in the traditional 'prayer' position at the centre of your chest. Breathe in and out. Become aware of the distribution of weight on each foot.

△ 3 On the next inbreath, stretch your arms up above your head and lean back slightly from your waist, looking up towards your hands.

YOGA EXPERTISE
Don't worry if when looking at the series of postures in the salute to the sun, you realize you cannot copy them exactly. Just do the best that you can, your chakras will still respond to the sequence, even if your yoga is not advanced.

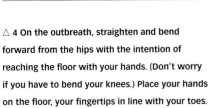

△ 4 On the outbreath, straighten and bend forward from the hips with the intention of reaching the floor with your hands. (Don't worry if you have to bend your knees.) Place your hands on the floor, your fingertips in line with your toes.

△ 5 On the next inbreath, send your right leg back so that your knee touches the floor and your toes are tucked under. Look upwards. If you have to shuffle your hands and feet around for stability, that is fine.

▽ 6 On the outbreath, lower your head and send your left leg back behind you to join the right leg. Allow your bottom to lift upwards away from the floor. Let your head drop down between your arms. Breathe in.

◁ 7 On the next outbreath, lower yourself, bending your knees so they touch the floor. Continue lowering your chest to the floor, then your chin. (Your hips stay off the floor.)

◁ 8 On the next inbreath, lower your hips, flatten your toes and lift your head and chest up, straightening your arms. Look upwards.

▽ 9 On the next outbreath, tuck your toes back under, pressing on your hands. Lift your hips so they are the highest part of you off the floor, and lower your head.

△ 10 Breathing in (lifting your chin so your knee doesn't catch it), bring your right foot forwards between your hands. (You may have to shuffle your body around a bit to do this.) Look upwards.

▽ 11 Breathing out, bring your right foot up to join your left, creating a forward bend. Keep your head low.

12 The next inbreath takes you upright again, leaning back slightly, with your hands above your head, looking upwards.

△ 13 On the outbreath, lower your arms. Repeat, sending the left leg back first (in step 6). Gradually build up the number of rounds from two to four, then six, and so on. Try to coordinate your breathing as you go. It will eventually come naturally as the postures themselves create an ebbing and flowing of the breath.

Glossary

Ajña: 'command', the brow chakra

Akasha: pure cosmic sound

Anahata: 'unstruck', the heart chakra

Anandakanda: the spiritual heart, containing our deepest hopes and wishes

Asanas: postures used in the practice of hatha yoga

Bija mantra: the sound that stimulates the energy of each chakra

Bindu: the cosmic seed, or origin of creation of the universe

Bodhicitta: complete openness of mind, acceptance

Chi: life-energy in traditional Chinese philosophy, the equivalent of prana

Chi Kung: Chinese energizing exercise using breathing control and visualization

Dharana: concentration

Dhyana: meditation

Hatha yoga: the physical aspect of yoga – the practice of a series of postures to aid spiritual development and health

Ida: left-hand nadi, carrying lunar energy

Kundalini: 'coiled up', the life-force, which resides in the base chakra; when

awakened and flowing freely, it brings realization and enlightenment

Manipura: 'city of gems', the solar plexus chakra

Mudras: positions of the hands designed to balance energy

Muladhara: 'foundation' or 'root', the base chakra

Nada: the quality of sound

Nadi: a channel of energy

Nadi sodhana: alternate nostril breathing, an exercise to balance energy

Niyama: observances of purity, contentment, effort, spiritual study, dedication to higher forces

Pingala: right-hand nadi, carrying solar energy

Prana: breath or wind, life-energy

Pranayama: breath control

Pratyahara: sense control

Raja yoga: 'the eight-fold path' that leads to meditation and enlightenment

Sahasrara: 'thousand-petalled', the crown chakra

Samadhi: 'union', comprehension

Sushumna: the central nadi, running parallel to the spine

Svadistana: 'sweetness', the sacral chakra

Tai Chi: Chinese martial art involving breath control and balanced movement

Vedas: body of sacred Hindu texts compiled from c.3000 BC

Vishuddha: 'pure', the throat chakra

Yama: general behaviour

Acknowledgements

All artworks created by Gary Walton, except for the following: Penny Brown, pp 13, 18, 19, 22; Samantha J Elmhurst, p15. Additional images were supplied by the following libraries:

The Artarchive/British Library, p10 and 14, Attitudes practised by Hindu devotees in Asanas and Matras 18th century; Fortean Picture Library, Pair of cosmic men of traditional Nepalese/Tibetan style depicting the seven chakras. Private collection, purchased in Nepal; Werner Forman Archive, p71, Ceramic tiles from the Alcazar of Seville, Islamic, 14th century.

Index